Also available from Macmillan

Read Me 2
A Poem for Every Day of the Year
Chosen by Gaby Morgan

Read Me and Laugh
A Funny Poem for Every Day of the Year
Chosen by Gaby Morgan

Read Me Out Loud!
A Poem to Rap, Chant, Whisper or Shout for Every
Day of the Year
Chosen by Nick Toczek and Paul Cookson

Read Me First
Poems for Younger Readers for
Every Day of the Year
Key Stages 1 and 2
Chosen by Louise Bolongaro

A Poem For Every Day Of The Year

Chosen by Gaby Morgan

MACMILLAN CHILDREN'S BOOKS

For Jonathan Douglas and for
Grant, Jude and Evie Weston

First published 1998 by Macmillan Children's Books

This edition published 2008 by Macmillan Children's Books
a division of Macmillan Publishers Limited
20 New Wharf Road, London N1 9RR
Basingstoke and Oxford
Associated companies throughout the world
www.panmacmillan.com

ISBN 978-0-330-45716-3

Typeset by SX Composing DTP, Rayleigh, Essex
Printed in the UK by CPI Mackays, Chatham ME5 8TD

Contents

January

February

March

April

May

June

July

August

September

October

November

December

January

The Months

January brings the snow,
Makes our feet and fingers glow.

February brings the rain,
Thaws the frozen lake again.

March brings breezes loud and shrill,
Stirs the dancing daffodil.

April brings the primrose sweet,
Scatters daisies at our feet.

May brings flocks of pretty lambs,
Skipping by their fleecy dams.

June brings tulips, lilies, roses,
Fills the children's hands with posies.

Hot July brings cooling showers,
Apricots and gillyflowers.

August brings the sheaves of corn,
Then the harvest home is borne.

Warm September brings the fruit,
Sportsmen then begin to shoot.

Fresh October brings the pheasant,
Then to gather nuts is pleasant.

Dull November brings the blast,
Then the leaves are whirling fast.

Chill December brings the sleet,
Blazing fire, and Christmas treat.

Sara Coleridge

Snow

In the gloom of whiteness,
In the great silence of snow,
A child was sighing
And bitterly saying: 'Oh,
They have killed a white bird up there on her nest,
The down is fluttering from her breast!'
And still it fell through the dusky brightness
On the child crying for the bird of the snow.

Edward Thomas

The Duck

Behold the duck.
It does not cluck.
A cluck it lacks.
It quacks.
It is specially fond
Of a puddle or pond.
When it dines or sups,
It bottoms ups.

Ogden Nash

My Rabbit

My rabbit
has funny habits.

When I say sit
he sits.

When he hears me call
he wags
his tail a bit.

When I throw a ball
he grabs it.

What a funny rabbit!

One day in the park
I swore I heard him bark.

John Agard

Tartary

If I were Lord of Tartary,
   Myself, and me alone,
My bed should be of ivory,
   Of beaten gold my throne;
And in my court should peacocks flaunt,
And in my forests tigers haunt,
And in my pools great fishes slant
     Their fins athwart the sun.

If I were Lord of Tartary,
   Trumpeters every day
To all my meals should summon me,
   And in my courtyards bray;
And in the evening lamps should shine,
Yellow as honey, red as wine,
While harp, and flute, and mandoline
     Made music sweet and gay.

If I were Lord of Tartary,
    I'd wear a robe of beads,
White, and gold, and green they'd be –
    And small and thick as seeds;
And ere should wane the morning star,
I'd don my robe and scimitar,
And zebras seven should draw my car
        Through Tartary's dark glades.

Lord of the fruits of Tartary,
    Her rivers silver-pale!
Lord of the hills of Tartary,
    Glen, thicket, wood, and dale!
Her flashing stars, her scented breeze,
Her trembling lakes, like foamless seas,
Her bird-delighting citron-trees,
        In every purple vale!

Walter de la Mare

The Meeting Place
(after Rubens: *The Adoration of the Magi*, 1634)

It was the arrival of the kings
that caught us unawares;
we'd look in on the woman in the barn,
curiosity you could call it,
something to do on a cold winter's night;
we'd wished her well –
that was the best we could do, she was in pain,
and the next thing we knew
she was lying on the straw
– the little there was of it –
and there was a baby in her arms.

It was, as I say, the kings
that caught us unawares . . .
Women have babies every other day,
not that we are there –
let's call it a common occurrence though,
giving birth. But kings
appearing in a stable with a
'Is this the place?' and kneeling,
each with his gift held out towards the child!

They didn't even notice us.
Their robes trailed on the floor,
rich, lined robes that money couldn't buy.
What must this child be
to bring kings from distant lands
with costly incense and gold?
What could a tiny baby make of that?

And what were we to make of
was it angels falling through the air,
entwined and falling as if from the rafters
to where the gaze of the kings met the child's
– assuming the child could see?
What would the mother do with the gift?
What would become of the child?
And we'll never admit there are angels
or that somewhere between
one man's eyes and another's
is a holy place, a space where a king could be
at one with a naked child,
at one with an astonished soldier.

Christopher Pilling

Why?

Why do cats
on winter nights
just as the goal of the year is about to be scored
appear at the window?

And why
having spilt tea
and finally
found key
and opened door
do they run away into the darkness?
Leaving me to wonder at their stupidity
And the final score.

Peter Dixon

My Mum's put me on the Transfer List

On Offer:
one nippy striker, ten years old
has scored seven goals this season
has nifty footwork and a big smile
knows how to dive in the penalty box
can get filthy and muddy within two minutes
guaranteed to wreck his kit each week
this is a FREE TRANSFER
but he comes with running expenses
weeks of washing shirts and shorts
socks and vests, a pair of trainers
needs to scoff huge amounts
of chips and burgers, beans and apples
pop and cola, crisps and oranges
endless packets of chewing gum.
This offer open until the end of the season
I'll have him back then
at least until the cricket starts.
Any takers?

David Harmer

Countdown

There are ten ghosts in the pantry,
There are nine upon the stairs,
There are eight ghosts in the attic,
There are seven on the chairs,
There are six within the kitchen,
There are five along the hall,
There are four upon the ceiling,
There are three upon the wall,
There are two ghosts on the carpet,
Doing things that ghosts will do,
There is one ghost right behind me
Who is oh so quiet . . . BOO.

Jack Prelutsky

First Morning

I was there on that first morning of creation
when heaven and earth occupied one space
and no one had heard of the human race.

I was there on that first morning of creation
when a river rushed from the belly of an egg
and a mountain rose from a golden yolk.

I was there on that first morning of creation
when the waters parted like magic cloth
and the birds shook feathers at the first joke.

John Agard

Hope

Sometimes when I'm lonely,
Don't know why,
Keep thinkin' I won't be lonely
By and by.

Langston Hughes

experiment

at school we're doing growing things
    with cress.
sprinkly seeds in plastic pots
    of cotton wool.

Kate's cress sits up on the sill
    she gives it water.
mine is shut inside the cupboard
    dark and dry.

now her pot has great big clumps
    of green
mine hasn't.
Mrs Martin calls it Science
    I call it mean.

Danielle Sensier

Little Robin Redbreast

Little Robin Redbreast
Sat upon a tree,
He sang merrily,
As merrily as could be.
He nodded with his head,
And his tail waggled he,
As little Robin Redbreast
Sat upon a tree.

Anon.

Jess

my cat is witless,
and rather plump –
but she has
certain capabilities.

she can open doors,
and climb trees
and make judicious displays
of affection.

She knows the cosiest places
to sleep,
and that the tin-opener
is her best friend.

I am not so limited, or so I like to think,
and I have more articulate ways
of expressing my emotions
than rolling over on the ground.

yet poetry remains
an unyielding cat-flap.
I don't understand why it is spaced out funny on the page like

      t

        h

          i

            s

Marion Simpson

Permit Holders Only

Daddy had an argument on Friday night,
With a man from outer space.
Daddy said, 'I don't care where you're from,
You're in my parking place!'

Colin McNaughton

I Saw

I saw a peacock with a fiery tail
I saw a blazing comet drop down hail
I saw a cloud with ivy circled round
I saw a sturdy oak creep on the ground
I saw an ant swallow up a whale
I saw a raging sea brim full of ale
I saw a Venice glass sixteen foot deep
I saw a well full of men's tears that weep
I saw their eyes all in a flame of fire
I saw a house as big as the moon and higher
I saw the sun even in the midst of night
I saw the man that saw this wondrous sight.

Anon.

Stopping by Woods on a Snowy Evening

Whose woods these are I think I know.
His house is in the village though;
He will not see me stopping here
To watch his woods fill up with snow.

My little horse must think it queer
To stop without a farmhouse near
Between the woods and frozen lake
The darkest evening of the year.

He gives his harness bells a shake
To ask if there is some mistake.
The only other sound's the sweep
Of easy wind and downy flake.

The woods are lovely, dark and deep,
But I have promises to keep,
And miles to go before I sleep,
And miles to go before I sleep.

Robert Frost

What is Pink?

What is pink? A rose is pink
By the fountain's brink.
What is red? A poppy's red
In its barley bed.
What is blue? The sky is blue
Where the clouds float through.
What is white? A swan is white
Sailing in the light.
What is yellow? Pears are yellow,
Rich and ripe and mellow.
What is green? The grass is green,
With small flowers between.
What is violet? Clouds are violet
In the summer twilight.
What is orange? Why, an orange,
Just an orange!

Christina Rossetti

Explorer

Two o'clock:
Let out of the back door of the house, our cat
Is practising the snow.

The layer of white makes a small, straight, crumbling cliff
Where we open the back door inwards. The cat
Sniffs it with suspicion, learns you can just about
Pat the flaking snow with a careful dab. Then,
A little bolder, he dints it with one whole foot
– and withdraws it, curls it as if slightly lame,

And looks down at it, oddly. The snow is
Different from anything else, not like
A rug, or a stretch of lino, or an armchair to claw upon
And be told to *Get off!*

The snow is peculiar, but not forbidden. The cat
Is welcome to go out in the snow. Does
The snow welcome the cat?
He thinks, looks, tries again.

Three paces out of the door, his white feet find
You sink a little way all the time, it is slow and cold, but it
Doesn't particularly hurt. Perhaps you can even enjoy it, as
   something new.
So he walks on, precisely, on the tips of very cautious
   paws . . .

Half-past three, the cat stretched warm indoors,
From the bedroom window we can see his explorations

– From door to fence, from fence to gate, from gate to wall
   to tree, and back,
Are long patterned tracks and trade-routes of round paw-
   marks
Which fresh snow is quietly filling.

Alan Brownjohn

There was an Old Man with a Beard

There was an Old Man with a beard,
Who said, 'It is just as I feared! –
    Two Owls and a Hen,
    Four Larks and a Wren,
Have all built their nests in my beard!'

Edward Lear

The Marrog

My desk's at the back of the class
And nobody, nobody knows
I'm a Marrog from Mars
With a body of brass
And seventeen fingers and toes.
Wouldn't they shriek if they knew
I've three eyes at the back of my head

And my hair is bright purple
My nose is deep blue
And my teeth are half-yellow, half-red?
My five arms are silver and spiked
With knives on them sharper than spears.
I could go back right now, if I liked –
And return in a million light-years.
I could gobble them all
For I'm seven foot tall
And I'm breathing green flames from my ears.
Wouldn't they yell if they knew,
If they guessed that a Marrog was here?
Ha-ha they haven't a clue –
Or wouldn't they tremble with fear!
'Look, look, a Marrog'
They'd all scream – and SMACK
The blackboard would fall and the ceiling would crack
And the teacher would faint, I suppose.
But I grin to myself, sitting right at the back
And nobody, nobody knows.

R.C. Scriven

Me and My Brother

Me and my brother,
we sit up in bed
doing my dad's sayings.
I go to bed first
and I'm just dozing off
and I hear a funny voice going:
'Never let me see you doing that again,'
and it's my brother
poking his finger out just like my dad
going:
'Never let me see you doing that again.'
And so I join in
and we're both going:
'Never
let
me
see
you
doing
that
again.'

So what happens next time I get into trouble
and my dad's telling me off?
He's going:
'Never let me see you doing that again.'
So I'm looking up at my dad
going,
'Sorry, Dad, sorry,'
and I suddenly catch sight of my brother's big red
face poking out from behind my dad.
And while my dad is poking me with his finger
in time with the words:
'Never
let
me
see
you
doing
that again,'
there's my brother doing just the same
behind my dad's back
just where I can see him
and he's saying the words as well
with his mouth without making a sound.

So I start laughing
and so my dad says,
'AND IT'S NO LAUGHING MATTER.'
Of course my brother knows that one as well
and he's going with his mouth:
'And it's no laughing matter.'

But my dad's not stupid.
He knows something's going on.
So he looks round
and there's my brother
with his finger poking out
just like my dad
and I'm standing there laughing.
Oh no
then we get into
REALLY BIG TROUBLE.

Michael Rosen

Happy Thought

The world is so full
  of a number of things,
I'm sure we should all
  be as happy as kings.

Robert Louis Stevenson

Tall Nettles

Tall nettles cover up, as they have done
These many springs, the rusty harrow, the plough
Long worn out, and the roller made of stone;
Only the elm butt tops the nettles now.

This corner of the farmyard I like most:
As well as any bloom upon a flower
I like the dust on the nettles, never lost
Except to prove the sweetness of a shower.

Edward Thomas

My Heart's in the Highlands

My heart's in the Highlands, my heart is not here;
My heart's in the Highlands a-chasing the deer;
Chasing the wild deer, and following the roe,
My heart's in the Highlands wherever I go.
Farewell to the Highlands, farewell to the North,
The birth-place of valour, the country of worth;
Wherever I wander, wherever I rove,
The hills of the Highlands for ever I love.

Farewell to the mountains, high covered with snow;
Farewell to the straths and green valleys below;
Farewell to the forests and wild-hanging woods;
Farewell to the torrents and loud-pouring floods.
My heart's in the Highlands, my heart is not here;
My heart's in the Highlands a-chasing the deer;
Chasing the wild deer, and following the roe,
My heart's in the Highlands, wherever I go.

Robert Burns

Kubla Khan

In Xanadu did Kubla Khan
A stately pleasure-dome decree:
Where Alph, the sacred river, ran
Through caverns measureless to man
  Down to a sunless sea.
So twice five miles of fertile ground
With walls and towers were girdled round:
And here were gardens bright with sinuous rills,
Where blossomed many an incense-bearing tree;
And here were forests ancient as the hills
Enfolding sunny spots of greenery.

But oh! that deep romantic chasm which slanted
Down the green hill athwart a cedarn cover!
A savage place! as holy and enchanted
As e'er beneath a waning moon was haunted
By woman wailing for her demon-lover!
And from this chasm, with ceaseless turmoil seething,
As if this earth in fast thick pants were breathing,
A mighty fountain momently was forced:
Amid whose swift half-intermitted burst
Huge fragments vaulted like rebounding hail,
Or chaffy grain beneath the thresher's flail;
And 'mid these dancing rocks at once and ever
It flung up momently the sacred river.
Five miles meandering with a mazy motion
Through wood and dale the sacred river ran,
Then reached the caverns measureless to man,
And sank in tumult to a lifeless ocean:
And 'mid this tumult Kubla heard from far
Ancestral voices prophesying war!

The shadow of the dome of pleasure
Floated midway on the waves;
Where was heard the mingled measure
From the fountain and the caves.
It was a miracle of rare device,
A sunny pleasure-dome with caves of ice!
A damsel with a dulcimer
In a vision once I saw:
It was an Abyssinian maid,
And on her dulcimer she played,
Singing of Mount Abora.
Could I revive within me
Her symphony and song,
To such a deep delight 'twould win me,
That with music loud and long,
I would build that dome in air,
That sunny dome! those caves of ice!
And all who heard should see them there,
And all should cry, Beware! Beware!
His flashing eyes, his floating hair!
Weave a circle round him thrice,
And close your eyes with holy dread,
For he on honey-dew hath fed,
And drunk the milk of Paradise.

S.T. Coleridge

Mum is Having a Baby!

Mum is having a baby!
I'm shocked! I'm all at sea!
What's she want another one for:
WHAT'S THE MATTER WITH ME!?

Colin McNaughton

You are Old, Father William

'You are old, Father William,' the young man said,
'And your hair has become very white;
And yet you incessantly stand on your head –
Do you think, at your age, it is right?'

'In my youth,' Father William replied to his son,
'I feared it might injure the brain;
But, now that I'm perfectly sure I have none,
Why, I do it again and again.'

'You are old,' said the youth, 'as I mentioned before,
And have grown most uncommonly fat;
Yet you turned a back-somersault in at the door –
Pray, what is the reason of that?'

'In my youth,' said the sage, as he shook his grey locks,
'I kept all my limbs very supple
By the use of this ointment – one shilling the box –
Allow me to sell you a couple?'

'You are old,' said the youth, 'and your jaws are too weak
For anything tougher than suet;
Yet you finished the goose, with the bones and the beak –
Pray, how did you manage to do it?'

'In my youth,' said his father, 'I took to the law,
And argued each case with my wife;
And the muscular strength, which it gave to my jaw,
Has lasted the rest of my life.'

'You are old,' said the youth, 'one would hardly suppose
That your eye was as steady as ever;
Yet you balanced an eel on the end of your nose –
What made you so awfully clever?'

'I have answered three questions, and that is enough,'
Said his father. 'Don't give yourself airs!
Do you think I can listen all day to such stuff?
Be off, or I'll kick you downstairs!'

Lewis Carroll

On the Pavement

Sauntering along alone I hear other busier footsteps behind
　me.
Not feeling threatened but awkward
I wonder, should I slow down my walking
and let them get by as soon as possible
or shall I imperceptibly quicken to a higher gear
before they are near enough to notice?
Ah, it's OK, it sounds like they've just fallen over.

John Hegley

A Poem for my Cat

You're black and sleek and beautiful
What a pity your best friends won't tell you
Your breath smells of Kit-E-Kat.

Adrian Henri

The Listeners

'Is there anybody there?' said the Traveller,
Knocking on the moonlit door;
And his horse in the silence champed the grasses
Of the forest's ferny floor;
And a bird flew up out of the turret,
Above the Traveller's head:
And he smote upon the door again a second time;
'Is there anybody there?' he said.
But no one descended to the Traveller;
No head from the leaf fringed sill
Leaned over and looked into his grey eyes,
Where he stood perplexed and still.
But only a host of phantom listeners
That dwelt in the lone house then
Stood listening in the quiet of the moonlight
To that voice from the world of men:
Stood thronging the faint moonbeams on the dark stair,
That goes down to the empty hall,
Hearkening in an air stirred and shaken
By the lonely Traveller's call.

And he felt in his heart their strangeness,
Their stillness answering his cry,
While his horse moved, cropping the dark turf,
'Neath the starred and leafy sky;
For he suddenly smote on the door, even
Louder, and lifted his head: –
'Tell them I came, and no one answered,
That I kept my word,' he said.
Never the least stir made the listeners,
Though every word he spake
Fell echoing through the shadowiness of the still house
From the one man left awake:
Ay, they heard his foot upon the stirrup,
And the sound of iron on stone,
And how the silence surged softly backward,
When the plunging hoofs were gone.

Walter de la Mare

February

A Slash of Blue

A slash of Blue –
A sweep of Gray –
Some scarlet patches on the way,
Compose an Evening Sky –
A little purple – slipped between
Some Ruby Trousers hurried on –
A Wave of Gold –
A Bank of Day –
This just makes out the Morning Sky.

Emily Dickinson

Pied Beauty

Glory be to God for dappled things –
   For skies of couple-colour as a brinded cow;
     For rose-moles all in stipple upon trout that swim;
Fresh-firecoal chestnut-falls; finches' wings;
   Landscape plotted and pieced – fold, fallow, and plough;
     And all trades, their gear and tackle and trim.

All things counter, original, spare, strange;
   Whatever is fickle, freckled (who knows how?)
     With swift, slow; sweet, sour; adazzle, dim;
He fathers-forth whose beauty is past change:
                Praise him.

Gerard Manley Hopkins

Tell Me the Truth About Love

Some say that love's a little boy,
    And some say it's a bird,
Some say it makes the world go round,
    And some say that's absurd,
And when I asked the man next-door,
    Who looked as if he knew,
His wife got very cross indeed,
    And said it wouldn't do.

Does it look like a pair of pyjamas,
    Or the ham in the temperance hotel?
Does its odour remind one of llamas,
    Or has it a comforting smell?
Is it prickly to touch as a hedge is,
    Or soft as eiderdown fluff?
Is it sharp or quite smooth at the edges?
    O tell me the truth about love.

Our history books refer to it
    In cryptic little notes,
It's quite a common topic on
    The Transatlantic boats;
I've found the subject mentioned in
    Accounts of suicides,
And even seen it scribbled on
    The backs of railway-guides.

Does it howl like a hungry Alsatian,
    Or boom like a military band?
Could one give a first-rate imitation
    On a saw or a Steinway Grand?
Is its singing at parties a riot?
    Does it only like Classical stuff?
Will it stop when one wants to be quiet?
    O tell me the truth about love.

I looked inside the summer-house;
    It wasn't ever there:
I tried the Thames at Maidenhead,
    And Brighton's bracing air.
I don't know what the blackbird sang,
    Or what the tulip said;
But it wasn't in the chicken-run,
    Or underneath the bed.

Can it pull extraordinary faces?
  Is it usually sick on a swing?
Does it spend all its times at the races,
  Or fiddling with pieces of string?
Has it views of its own about money?
  Does it think Patriotism enough?
Are its stories vulgar but funny?
  O tell me the truth about love.

When it comes, will it come without warning
  Just as I'm picking my nose?
Will it knock on my door in the morning,
  Or tread in the bus on my toes?
Will it come like a change in the weather?
  Will its greeting be courteous or rough?
Will it alter my life altogether?
  O tell me the truth about love.

W.H. Auden

Measles in the Ark

THE night it was horribly dark,
The measles broke out in the Ark;
Little Japheth, and Shem, and all the young Hams,
Were screaming at once for potatoes and clams.
And 'What shall I do,' said poor Mrs Noah,
'All alone by myself in this terrible shower?
I know what I'll do: I'll step down in the hold,
And wake up a lioness grim and old,
And tie her close to the children's door,
And give her a ginger-cake to roar
At the top of her voice for an hour or more;
And I'll tell the children to cease their din,
Or I'll let that grim old party in,
To stop their squeazles and likewise their measles.'
She practised this with the greatest success:
She was everyone's grandmother, I guess.

Susan Coolidge

Creative Writing

My story on Monday began:
Mountainous seas crashed on the cliffs,
And the desolate land grew wetter . . .
The teacher wrote a little note: *Remember the capital letter!*

My poem on Tuesday began:
Red tongues of fire,
Licked higher and higher
From smoking Etna's top . . .
The teacher wrote a little note: *Where is your full stop?*

My story on Wednesday began:
Through the lonely, pine-scented wood
There twists a hidden path . . .
The teacher wrote a little note: *Start a paragraph!*

My poem on Thursday began:
The trembling child,
Eyes dark and wild,
Frozen midst the fighting . . .
The teacher wrote a little note: *Take care – untidy writing!*

My story on Friday began:
   The boxer bruised and bloody lay,
   His eye half closed and swollen . . .
The teacher wrote a little note: *Use a semi-colon!*

Next Monday my story will begin:
   Once upon a time . . .

                      Gervase Phinn

The Magic Box

I will put in the box

the swish of a silk sari on a summer night,
fire from the nostrils of a Chinese dragon,
the tip of a tongue touching a tooth.

I will put in the box

a snowman with a rumbling belly,
a sip of the bluest water from Lake Lucerne,
a leaping spark from an electric fish.

I will put in the box

three violet wishes spoken in Gujarati,
the last joke of an ancient uncle
and the first smile of a baby.

I will put in the box

a fifth season and a black sun,
a cowboy on a broomstick
and a witch on a white horse.

My box is fashioned from ice and gold and steel,
with stars on the lid and secrets in the corners.
Its hinges are the toe joints
of dinosaurs.

I shall surf on my box
on the great high-rolling breaks of the wild Atlantic,
then wash ashore on a yellow beach
the colour of the sun.

Kit Wright

What's in There?

What's in there?
　Gold and money.
Where's my share of it?
　The mouse ran away with it.
Where's the mouse?
　In her house.

Where's the house?
　In the wood.
Where's the wood?
　The fire burnt it.
Where's the fire?
　The water quenched it.

Where's the water?
   The brown bull drank it.
Where's the brown bull?
   At the back of Birnie's Hill.
Where's Birnie's Hill?
   All clad with snow.
Where's the snow?
   The sun melted it.
Where's the sun?
   High, high up in the air.

Anon.

When a Knight Won his Spurs

When a knight won his spurs, in the stories of old,
He was gentle and brave, he was gallant and bold;
With a shield on his arm and a lance in his hand
For God and for valour he rode through the land.

No charger have I, and no sword by my side,
Yet still to adventure and battle I ride,
Though back into storyland giants have fled,
And the knights are no more and the dragons are dead.

Let faith be my shield and let joy be my steed
'Gainst the dragons of anger, the ogres of greed;
And let me set free, with the sword of my youth,
From the castle of darkness the power of the truth.

Jan Struther

Daddy Fell into the Pond

Everyone grumbled. The sky was grey.
We had nothing to do and nothing to say.
We were nearing the end of a dismal day.
And there seemed to be nothing beyond,
   Then
      Daddy fell into the pond!

And everyone's face grew merry and bright,
And Timothy danced for sheer delight.
'Give me the camera, quick, oh quick!
He's crawling out of the duckweed!' Click!

Then the gardener suddenly slapped his knee,
And doubled up, shaking silently,
And the ducks all quacked as if they were daft,
And it sounded as if the old drake laughed.
Oh, there wasn't a thing that didn't respond
  When
    Daddy fell into the pond!

Alfred Noyes

The Piper

Piping down the valleys wild,
Piping songs of pleasant glee,
On a cloud I saw a child,
And he laughing said to me:

'Pipe a song about a lamb!'
So I piped with merry cheer.
'Piper, pipe that song again;'
So I piped: he wept to hear.

'Drop thy pipe, thy happy pipe;
Sing thy songs of happy cheer.'
So I sung the same again,
While he wept with joy to hear.

'Piper, sit thee down and write
In a book that all may read.'
So he vanished from my sight,
And I plucked a hollow reed.

And I made a rural pen,
And I stained the water clear,
And I wrote my happy songs
Every child may joy to hear.

William Blake

There Once Was a Man

There once was a man
Called Knocketty Ned
Who wore a cat
On top of his head.
Upstairs, downstairs,
The whole world knew
Wherever he went
The cat went too.

He wore it at work,
He wore it at play,
He wore it to town
On market-day,
And for fear it should rain
Or the snowflakes fly
He carried a brolly
To keep it dry.

He never did fret
Nor fume because
He always knew
Just where it was.
'And when,' said Ned,
'In my bed I lie
There's no better nightcap
Money can buy.'

'There's no better bonnet
To be found,'
Said Knocketty Ned,
'The world around.
And furthermore
Was there ever a hat
As scared a mouse
Or scared a rat?'

Did ever you hear
Of a tale like that
As Knocketty Ned's
And the tale of his cat?

Charles Causley

Montana Born

I saw her first through wavering candlelight,
My sister in her cradle, one hour old;
Outside, the snow was drifting through the night,
But she lay warm, oblivious to the cold.

Her eyes were closed, the half-moist wisps of hair,
A honey harvest on her wrinkled head,
The smile upon her face as if she was elsewhere,
But knew the land she had inherited.

My mother there at peace, her labour done,
Their greyness gone, her cheeks were coralline,
She welcomed me, her wondering first-born son
And placed my sister's new-nailed hand in mine.

I looked through the freezing window pane,
The whitening acre bare and stretching far
That nine months hence would heave with swelling grain,
And over every distant peak a star.

And she, my winter sister, does she know
That all this homely countryside is hers,
Where once were warring Sioux and buffalo,
And covered waggons full of travellers?

But I will tell her the Indian tales,
And show her grass-high fields, and sugar beet,
We'll ride all day along the western trails,
Missouri River glinting at our feet.

Montana born, she'll sleep beneath these beams,
And learn the simple ways, and say her prayers,
And even now she may see in her dreams
Another boy come climbing up the stairs.

Leonard Clark

The Lion and the Unicorn

The lion and the unicorn
Were fighting for the crown;
The lion beat the unicorn
All round the town.

Some gave them white bread,
And some gave them brown;
Some gave them plum-cake,
And drummed them out of town.

Anon.

Valentine Poem

If I were a poet
I'd write poems for you.
If I were a musician,
Music too.
But as I'm only an average man
I give you my love
As best what I can.

If I were a sculptor
I'd sculpt you in a stone.
An osteopath,
Work myself to the bone.
But as I'm just a man in the street
I give you my love,
Lay my heart at your feet
    (ugh!)

If I were an orator
I'd make pretty speeches.
An oil tanker,
Break up on your beaches.
But as I'm just an ordinary Joe
I send you my love,
As best what I know.

Roger McGough

How do I love thee?

How do I love thee? Let me count the ways,
I love thee to the depth and breadth and height
My soul can reach, when feeling out of sight
For the ends of Being and ideal Grace.

I love thee to the level of everyday's
Most quiet need, by sun and candlelight.
I love thee freely, as men strive for Right;
I love thee purely, as they turn from Praise.

I love thee with the passion put to use
In my old griefs, and with my childhood's faith.
I love thee with a love I seemed to lose

With my lost saints – I love thee with the breath,
Smiles, tears, of all my life! – and, if God choose
I shall but love thee better after death.

Elizabeth Barrett Browning

New Shoes

My shoes are new and squeaky shoes,
They're shiny, creaky shoes,
I wish I had my leaky shoes
That my mother threw away.

I liked my old brown leaky shoes
Much better than these creaky shoes,
These shiny, creaky, squeaky shoes
I've got to wear today.

Anon.

The Uncertainty of the Poet

I am a poet.
I am very fond of bananas.

I am bananas.
I am very fond of a poet.

I am a poet of bananas.
I am very fond,

A fond poet of 'I am, I am' –
Very bananas,

Fond of 'Am I bananas,
Am I?' – a very poet.

Bananas of a poet!
Am I fond? Am I very?

Poet bananas! I am.
I am fond of a 'very'.

I am of very fond bananas.
Am I a poet?

Wendy Cope

Three Little Ghostesses

Three little ghostesses,
Sitting on postesses,
Eating buttered toastesses,
Greasing their fistesses,
Up to the wristesses,
Oh, what beastesses
To make such feastesses!

Anon.

Shining Things

I love all shining things –
          the lovely moon,
The silver stars at night,
          gold sun at noon.
A glowing rainbow in
          a stormy sky,
Or bright clouds hurrying
          when wind goes by.

I love the glow-worm's elf-light
          in the lane,
And leaves a-shine with glistening
          drops of rain,
The glinting wings of bees,
          and butterflies,
My purring pussy's green
          and shining eyes.

I love the street-lamps shining
　　　　through the gloom,
Tall candles lighted in
　　　　a shadowy room,
New-tumbled chestnuts from
　　　　the chestnut tree,
And gleaming fairy bubbles
　　　　blown by me.

I love the shining buttons
　　　　on my coat,
I love the bright beads round
　　　　my mother's throat.
I love the coppery flames
　　　　of red and gold,
That cheer and comfort me,
　　　　when I'm a-cold.

The beauty of all shining things
　　　　is yours and mine,
It was a *lovely* thought of God
　　　　to make things shine.

Elizabeth Gould

Rover
for David Ross

I have a pet oyster called Rover.
He lives in the bathroom sink
and is never any trouble:
no birdseed or tins of Kennomeat,
no cat-litter.
We don't need to take him for walks,
we don't need an oyster-flap in the back door.

He doesn't bark
or sing,
just lies in the sink
and never says a thing.
Sometimes,
when he feels irritable,
he grits his teeth
and produces a little pearl.

At night,
we tuck him up snug in his oyster-bed
until the bathroom tide comes in
in the morning.

Sometimes
I look at Rover and say
'The world's your lobster,
Rover', I say.

Adrian Henri

My Puppy

It's funny
my puppy
knows just how I feel.

When I'm happy
he's yappy
and squirms like an eel.

When I'm grumpy
he's slumpy
and stays at my heel.

It's funny
my puppy
knows such a great deal.

Aileen Fisher

Early Spring

Daffodils shiver,
huddle away from the wind,
like people waiting at a bus-stop.

Adrian Henri

Lavender's Blue

Lavender's blue, dilly dilly, lavender's green,
When I am king, dilly dilly, you shall be queen.
Who told you so, dilly dilly, who told you so?
'Twas mine own heart, dilly dilly, that told me so.

Call up your men, dilly dilly, set them to work,
Some with a rake, dilly dilly, some with a fork,
Some to make hay, dilly dilly, some to thresh corn,
Whilst you and I, dilly dilly, keep ourselves warm.

Anon.

Today

Today I will not live up to my potential.
Today I will not relate well to my peer group.
Today I will not contribute in class.
   I will not volunteer one thing.
Today I will not strive to do better.
Today I will not achieve or adjust or grow enriched
   or get involved.
I will not put up my hand even if the teacher is wrong
   and I can prove it.

Today I might eat the eraser off my pencil.
I'll look at the clouds.
I'll be late.
I don't think I'll wash.

I need a rest.

Jean Little

Happy the Man

Happy the man, and happy he alone,
  He who can call today his own;
He who, secure within, can say,
  Tomorrow, do thy worst, for I have lived today.

John Dryden

What Teachers Wear in Bed!

It's anybody's guess
what teachers wear in bed at night,
so we held a competition
to see if any of us were right.

We did a spot of research,
although some of them wouldn't say,
but it's probably something funny
as they look pretty strange by day.

Our headteacher's quite old-fashioned,
he wears a Victorian nightshirt,
our sports teacher wears her tracksuit
and sometimes her netball skirt.

That new teacher in the Infants,
wears bedsocks with see-through pyjamas,
our deputy head wears a T-shirt
he brought back from the Bahamas.

We asked our secretary what she wore
but she shooed us out of her room,
and our teacher said, her favourite nightie
and a splash of expensive perfume.

And Mademoiselle, who teaches French,
is really very rude,
she whispered, 'Alors! Don't tell a soul,
but I sleep in the . . . back bedroom!'

Brian Moses

A Cradle Song

Golden slumbers kiss your eyes,
Smiles awake you when you rise.
Sleep, pretty wantons, do not cry,
And I will sing a lullaby:
Rock them, rock them, lullaby.

Care is heavy, therefore sleep you;
You are care, and care must keep you.
Sleep, pretty wantons, do not cry,
And I will sing a lullaby:
Rock them, rock them, lullaby.

Thomas Dekker

You Can't Be That

I told them:
When I grow up
I'm not going to be a scientist
Or someone who reads the news on TV.
No, a million birds will fly through me.
I'M GOING TO BE A TREE.

They said,
You can't be that. No, you can't be that.

I told them:
When I grow up
I'm not going to be an airline pilot,
A dancer, a lawyer or an MC.
No, huge whales will swim in me.
I'M GOING TO BE AN OCEAN!

They said,
You can't be that. No, you can't be that.

I told them:
I'm not going to be a DJ,
A computer programmer, a musician or beautician.
No, streams will flow through me, I'll be the home of eagles;
I'll be full of nooks, crannies, valleys and fountains.
I'M GOING TO BE A RANGE OF MOUNTAINS!

They said,
You can't be that. No, you can't be that.

I asked them:
Just what do you think I am?
Just a child, they said,
And children always become
At least one of the things
We want them to be.

They do not understand me.
I'll be a stable if I want, smelling of fresh hay,
I'll be a lost glade in which unicorns still play.
They do not realize I can fulfil any ambition.
They do not realize among them
Walks a magician.

Brian Patten

If it's a leap year turn to page 470 for 29 February

March

A Change in the Year

It is the first mild day of March:
  Each minute sweeter than before,
The redbreast sings from the tall larch
  That stands beside our door.

There is a blessing in the air,
  Which seems a sense of joy to yield
To the bare trees, and mountains bare;
  And grass in the green field.

William Wordsworth

The Fight of the Year

'And there goes the bell for the third month
and Winter comes out of its corner looking groggy
Spring leads with a left to the head
followed by a sharp right to the body
    daffodils
    primroses
    crocuses
    snowdrops
    lilacs
    violets
    pussywillow
Winter can't take much more punishment
and Spring shows no signs of tiring
    tadpoles
    squirrels
    baalambs
    badgers
    bunny rabbits
    mad march hares
    horses and hounds

Spring is merciless
Winter won't go the full twelve rounds
   bobtail clouds
   scallywag winds
   the sun
   a pavement artist
   in every town
A left to the chin
and Winter's down!
   tomatoes
   radish
   cucumber
   onions
   beetroot
   celery
   and any
   amount
   of lettuce
   for dinner
Winter's out for the count
Spring is the winner!'

Roger McGough

Monday's Child

Monday's child is fair of face,
Tuesday's child is full of grace,
Wednesday's child is full of woe,
Thursday's child has far to go,
Friday's child is loving and giving,
Saturday's child works hard for a living,
But the child that is born on the Sabbath day
Is bonny, and blithe, and good, and gay.

Anon.

March

Dear March – Come In –
How glad I am –
I hoped for you before –
Put down your Hat –
You must have walked –
How out of Breath you are –
Dear March, how are you, and the Rest –
Did you leave Nature well –
Oh March, Come right up stairs with me –
I have so much to tell –

I got your Letter, and the Birds –
The Maples never knew that you were coming – till I called
I declare – how Red their Faces grew –
But March, forgive me – and
All those Hills you left for me to Hue –
There was no Purple suitable –
You took it all with you –

Who knocks? That April.
Lock the Door –
I will not be pursued –
He stayed away a Year to call
When I am occupied –
But trifles look so trivial
As soon as you have come

That Blame is just as dear as Praise
And Praise as mere as Blame –

Emily Dickinson

I'm not frightened of Pussy Cats

I'm not frightened of Pussy Cats,
They only eat up mice and rats,
But a Hippopotamus
Could eat the Lotofus!

Spike Milligan

The Paint Box

'Cobalt and umber and ultramarine,
Ivory black and emerald green –
What shall I paint to give pleasure to you?'
'Paint for me somebody utterly new.'

'I have painted you tigers in crimson and white.'
'The colours were good and you painted aright.'
'I have painted the cook and camel in blue
And a panther in purple.' 'You painted them true.

Now mix me a colour that nobody knows,
And paint me a country where nobody goes,
And put in it people a little like you,
Watching a unicorn drinking the dew.'

E.V. Rieu

Can't be bothered to think of a title

When they make slouching in the chair
an Olympic sport
I'll be there.

When they give out a cup
for refusing to get up
I'll win it every year.

When they hand out the gold
for sitting by the fire
I'll leave the others in the cold,

and when I'm asked to sign my name
in the Apathetic Hall of Fame
I won't go.

Ian McMillan

The Browny Hen

A browny hen sat on her nest
  With a hey-ho for the springtime!
Seven brown eggs 'neath her downy breast,
  With a hey-ho for the springtime!

A brown hen clucks all day from dawn,
  With a hey-ho for the springtime!
She's seven wee chicks as yellow as corn,
  With a hey-ho for the springtime!

Irene F. Fawsey

Easter Monday
(*In Memoriam E.T.*)

In the last letter that I had from France
You thanked me for the silver Easter egg
Which I had hidden in the box of apples
You liked to munch beyond all other fruit.
You found the egg the Monday before Easter,
And said, 'I will praise Easter Monday now –
It was such a lovely morning'. Then you spoke
Of the coming battle and said, 'This is the eve.
Good-bye. And may I have a letter soon.'

That Easter Monday was a day for praise,
It was such a lovely morning. In our garden
We sowed our earliest seeds, and in the orchard
The apple-bud was ripe. It was the eve.
There are three letters that you will not get.

Eleanor Farjeon

Eletelephony

Once there was an elephant,
Who tried to use the telephant –
No! No! I mean an elephone
Who tried to use the telephone –
(Dear me! I am not certain quite
That even now I've got it right.)

Howe'er it was, he got his trunk
Entangled in the telephunk;
The more he tried to get it free,
The louder buzzed the telephee –
(I fear I'd better drop the song
Of elephop and telephong!)

Laura E. Richards

I Asked the Little Boy who Cannot See

I asked the little boy who cannot see,
'And what is colour like?'
'Why, green,' said he,
'Is like the rustle when the wind blows through
The forest; running water, that is blue;
And red is like a trumpet sound; and pink
Is like the smell of roses; and I think
That purple must be like a thunderstorm;
And yellow is like something soft and warm;
And white is a pleasant stillness when you lie
And dream.'

Anon.

Grannie

I stayed with her when I was six then went
To live elsewhere when I was eight years old.
For ages I remembered her faint scent
Of lavender, the way she'd never scold
No matter what I'd done, and most of all
The way her smile seemed, somehow, to enfold
My whole world like a warm, protective shawl.

I knew that I was safe when she was near,
She was so tall, so wide, so large, she would
Stand mountainous between me and my fear,
Yet oh, so gentle, and she understood
Every hope and dream I ever had.
She praised me lavishly when I was good,
But never punished me when I was bad.

Years later war broke out and I became
A soldier and was wounded while in France.
Back home in hospital, still very lame,
I realized suddenly that circumstance
Had brought me close to that small town where she
Was living still. And so I seized the chance
To write and ask if she could visit me.

She came. And I still vividly recall
The shock that I received when she appeared
That dark cold day. Huge grannie was so small!
A tiny, frail, old lady. It was weird.
She hobbled through the ward to where I lay
And drew quite close and, hesitating, peered.
And then she smiled: and love lit up the day.

Vernon Scannell

Betty Botter

Betty Botter bought some butter,
But, she said, this butter's bitter;
If I put it in my batter,
It will make my batter bitter,
But a bit of better butter
Will make my batter better.
So she bought a bit of butter
Better than her bitter butter,
And she put it in her batter,
And it made her batter better,
So 'twas better Betty Botter
Bought a bit of better butter.

Anon.

Burying the Dog in the Garden

When we buried
the dog in
the garden on
the grave we put
a cross and
the tall man
next door was
cross.
'Animals have no
souls,' he said.
'They must have animal
souls,' we said. 'No,'
he said and
shook his head.
'Do you need a
soul to go
to Heaven?' we
asked. He nodded
his head. 'Yes,'
he said.

'That means my
hamster's not
in Heaven,' said
Kevin. 'Nor is
my dog,' I said.
'My cat could sneak
in anywhere,' said
Clare. And we thought
what a strange place Heaven
must be with
nothing to stroke
for eternity.
We were all
seven.
We decided we
did not want to
go to Heaven.
For that the
tall man next
door is to blame.

Brian Patten

back yard

Sun in the back yard
Grows lazy,

Dozing on the porch steps
All morning,

Getting up and nosing
About corners,

Gazing into an empty
Flowerpot,

Later easing over the grass
For a nap,

Unless
Someone hangs out the wash –

Which changes
Everything to a rush and clap

Of wet
Cloth, and fresh wind

And sun
Wide awake in the white sheets.

Valerie Worth

The Happy Child

I saw this day sweet flowers grow thick –
But not one like the child did pick.

I heard the pack-hounds in green park –
But no dog like the child heard bark.

I heard this day bird after bird –
But not one like the child has heard.

A hundred butterflies saw I –
But not one like the child saw fly.

I saw horses roll in grass –
But no horse like the child saw pass.

My world this day has lovely been –
But not like what the child has seen.

W.H. Davies

The Frog

What a wonderful bird the frog are –
When he sit, he stand almost;
When he hop, he fly almost.
He ain't got no sense hardly;
He ain't got no tail hardly either.
When he sit, he sit on what he ain't got – almost.

Anon.

Brendon Gallacher
(for my brother, Maxie)

He was seven and I was six, my Brendon Gallacher.
He was Irish and I was Scottish, my Brendon Gallacher.
His father was in prison; he was a cat burglar.
My father was a communist party full-time worker.
He has six brothers and I had one, my Brendon Gallacher.

He would hold my hand and take me by the river
Where we'd talk all about his family being poor.
He'd get his mum out of Glasgow when he got older.
A wee holiday some place nice. Some place far.
I'd tell my mum about my Brendon Gallacher.

How his mum drank and his daddy was a cat burglar.
And she'd say, 'Why not have him round to dinner?'
No, no, I'd say, he's got big holes in his trousers.
I like meeting him by the burn in the open air.
Then one day after we'd been friends two years,

One day when it was pouring and I was indoors,
My mum says to me, 'I was talking to Mrs Moir
Who lives next door to your Brendon Gallacher
Didn't you say his address was 24 Novar?
She says there are no Gallachers at 24 Novar

There never have been any Gallachers next door.'
And he died then, my Brendon Gallacher,
Flat out on my bedroom floor, his spiky hair,
His impish grin, his funny flapping ear.
Oh Brendon, oh my Brendon Gallacher.

Jackie Kay

The Dying Airman

A handsome young airman lay dying,
And as on the aerodrome he lay,
To the mechanics who round him came sighing,
The last dying words did he say:

'Take the cylinders out of my kidneys,
The connecting-rod out of my brain,
Take the cam-shaft from out of my backbone,
And assemble the engine again.'

Anon.

A Morning Song
For the First Day of Spring

Morning has broken
Like the first morning,
Blackbird has spoken
    Like the first bird.
Praise for the singing!
Praise for the morning!
Praise for them, springing
    From the first Word.

Sweet the rain's new fall
Sunlit from heaven,
Like the first dewfall
  In the first hour.
Praise for the sweetness
Of the wet garden,
Spring in completeness
  From the first shower.

Mine is the sunlight!
Mine is the morning
Born of the one light
  Eden saw play.
Praise with elation,
Praise every morning
Spring's re-creation
  Of the First Day!

Eleanor Farjeon

Pippa's Song

The year's at the spring;
The day's at the morn;
Morning's at seven;
The hill-side's dew-pearled;
The lark's on the wing;
The snail's on the thorn;
God's in His heaven –
All's right with the world!

Robert Browning

Dear Mum,

While you were out
a cup went and broke itself,
a crack appeared in the blue vase
your great-great grandad
brought back from Mr Ming in China.
Somehow, without me even turning on the tap,
the sink mysteriously overflowed.
A strange jam-stain,
about the size of a boy's hand,
appeared on the kitchen wall.
I don't think we will ever discover
exactly how the cat
managed to turn on the washing-machine
(especially from the inside),
or how Sis's pet rabbit went and mistook
the waste-disposal unit for a burrow.
I can tell you I was scared when,
as if by magic,
a series of muddy footprints
appeared on the new white carpet.
I was being good
(honest)
but I think the house is haunted so,

knowing you're going to have a fit,
I've gone over to Gran's for a bit.

Brian Patten

The English Succession

The Norman Conquest all historians fix
To the year of Christ, one thousand sixty-six.
Two Wills, one Henry, Stephen, Kings are reckoned;
Then rose Plantagenet in Henry second.
First Richard, John, third Henry, Edwards three,
And second Richard in one line we see.
Fourth, fifth, and sixth Lancastrian Henrys reign;
Then Yorkist Edwards two, and Richard slain.
Next Tudor comes in seventh Henry's right,
Who the red rose engrafted on the white.
Eighth Henry, Edward sixth, first Mary, Bess;
Then Scottish Stuart's right the peers confess.
James, double Charles, a second James expelled;
With Mary, Will; then Anne the sceptre held.
Last, Brunswick's issue has two Georges given;
Late may the second pass from earth to heaven!

Anon.

Forgiven

I found a little beetle, so that Beetle was his name,
And I called him Alexander and he answered just the same.
I put him in a match-box, and I kept him all the day . . .
And Nanny let my beetle out –

   Yes, Nanny let my beetle out –

   She went and let my beetle out –

      And Beetle ran away.

She said she didn't mean it, and I never said she did,
She said she wanted matches and she just took off the lid,
She said that she was sorry, but it's difficult to catch
An excited sort of beetle you've mistaken for a match.

She said that she was sorry, and I really mustn't mind,
As there's lots and lots of beetles which she's certain we
   could find,
If we looked about the garden for the holes where beetles
   hid –
And we'd get another match-box and write BEETLE on the
   lid.

We went to all the places which a beetle might be near,
And we made the sort of noises which a beetle likes to hear,
And I saw a kind of something, and I gave a sort of shout:
'A beetle-house and Alexander Beetle is coming out!'

It was Alexander Beetle I'm as certain as can be,
And he had a sort of look as if he thought it must be Me,
And he had a sort of look as if he thought he ought to say:
'I'm very very sorry that I tried to run away.'

And Nanny's very sorry too for you-know-what-she-did,
And she's writing ALEXANDER very blackly on the lid.
So Nan and Me are friends, because it's difficult to catch
An excited Alexander you've mistaken for a match.

A.A. Milne

A Fairy Song

Over hill, over dale,
    Thorough bush, thorough brier,
Over park, over pale,
    Thorough flood, thorough fire!
I do wander everywhere,
Swifter than the moon's sphere;
And I serve the fairy queen,
To dew her orbs upon the green;
The cowslips tall her pensioners be;
In their gold coats spots you see;
Those be rubies, fairy favours,
In those freckles live their savours:
I must go seek some dewdrops here,
And hang a pearl in every cowslip's ear.

William Shakespeare

Walking a Friend's Dog
Devon, Midnight

I just can't see,
don't know
where anything is.

I must *imagine* hedges,
the sky, the lane ahead.
Tonight is as black
as loudspeakers,
as peppercorns, as rain-
soaked soil, as black
as a mole's eyesight
underground.

It doesn't bother the dog.
He can see with his wet
black nose, snuffling
at hedges. He can tell
where a fox has shouldered
through, can hear
the fieldmice scratch.

Tonight is black
as lofts, as cupboards
under stairs, so dark
I'm scared . . .

me . . . a grown man
from the phosphorescent city . . .
asking '*Is it time to turn back home?*
Are you still there?'

Matt Simpson

Loveliest of trees

Loveliest of trees, the cherry now
Is hung with bloom along the bough,
And stands about the woodland ride
Wearing white for Eastertide.

Now, of my threescore years and ten,
Twenty will not come again,
And take from seventy springs a score,
It only leaves me fifty more.

And since to look at things in bloom
Fifty springs are little room,
About the woodlands I will go
To see the cherry hung with snow.

A.E. Housman

I Had a Little Cat

I had a little cat called Tim Tom Tay,
I took him to town on market day,
I combed his whiskers, I brushed his tail,
I wrote on a label, 'Cat for Sale.
Knows how to deal with rats and mice.
Two pounds fifty. Bargain price.'

But when the people came to buy
I saw such a look in Tim Tom's eye
That it was clear as clear could be
I couldn't sell Tim for a fortune's fee.
I was shamed and sorry, I'll tell you plain,
And I took home Tim Tom Tay again.

Charles Causley

The Donkey

When fishes flew and forests walked
  And figs grew upon thorn,
Some moment when the moon was blood
  Then surely I was born.

With monstrous head and sickening cry
  And ears like errant wings,
The devil's walking parody
  Of all four-footed things.

The tattered outlaw of the earth,
  Of ancient crooked will;
Starve, scourge, deride me: I am dumb,
  I keep my secret still.

Fools! For I also had my hour,
  One far fierce hour and sweet.
There was a shout about my ears,
  And palms before my feet.

G.K. Chesterton

Matilda
who told lies, and was burned to death

Matilda told such Dreadful Lies,
It made one Gasp and Stretch one's Eyes;
Her Aunt, who, from her Earliest Youth,
Had kept a Strict Regard for Truth,
Attempted to Believe Matilda:
The effort very nearly killed her,
And would have done so, had not She
Discovered this Infirmity.
For once, towards the Close of Day,
Matilda, growing tired of play,
And finding she was left alone,
Went tiptoe to the Telephone
And summoned the Immediate Aid
Of London's Noble Fire-Brigade.
Within an hour the Gallant Band
Were pouring in on every hand,
From Putney, Hackney Downs and Bow,
With Courage high and Hearts a-glow
They galloped, roaring through the Town,
'Matilda's House is Burning Down!'
Inspired by British Cheers and Loud
Proceeding from the Frenzied Crowd,

They ran their ladders through a score
Of windows on the Ball Room Floor;
And took Peculiar Pains to Souse
The Pictures up and down the House,
Until Matilda's Aunt succeeded
In showing them they were not needed
And even then she had to pay
To get the Men to go away!

It happened that a few Weeks later
Her Aunt was off to the Theatre
To see that Interesting Play
The Second Mrs Tanqueray.
She had refused to take her Niece
To hear this Entertaining Piece:
A Deprivation Just and Wise
To Punish her for Telling Lies.
That Night a Fire *did* break out –
You should have heard Matilda Shout!
You should have heard her Scream and Bawl,
And throw the window up and call
To People passing in the Street –
(The rapidly increasing Heat
Encouraging her to obtain
Their confidence) – but all in vain!
For every time She shouted 'Fire!'
They only answered 'Little Liar!'
And therefore when her Aunt returned,
Matilda, and the House, were Burned.

Hilaire Belloc

Mr Khan's Shop

is dark and beautiful.
There are parathas,

garam masala,
nan breads full of fruit.

There are bhajees, samosas, dhal,
garlic, ground cumin seeds.

Shiny emerald chillies
lie like incendiary bombs.

There are bhindi in sacks,
aaloo to eat with hot puris

and mango pickle. There's
rice, yoghurt,

cucumber and mint –
raitha to cool the tongue.

Sometimes you see
where the shop darkens

Mr Khan, his wife
and their children

round the table.
The smells have come alive.

He serves me
puppadums, smiles,

re-enters the dark.
Perhaps one day

he'll ask me to dine with them:
bhajees, samosas, pakoras,

coriander, dhall.
I'll give him this poem: *Sit down*

young man, he'll say
and eat your words.

Fred Sedgwick

April

The Cuckoo

In April
Come he will,
In flow'ry May
He sings all day,
In leafy June
He changes his tune,
In bright July
He's ready to fly,
In August
Go he must.

Anon.

Secret

Tell me your secret.
I promise not to tell.
I'll guard it safely at the bottom of a well.

Tell me your secret.
Tell me, tell me, please.
I won't breathe a word, not even to the bees.

Tell me your secret.
It will be a pebble in my mouth.
Not even the sea can make me spit it out.

John Agard

Daffodils

I wander'd lonely as a cloud
   That floats on high o'er vales and hills,
When all at once I saw a crowd,
   A host of golden daffodils;
Beside the lake, beneath the trees,
Fluttering and dancing in the breeze.

Continuous as the stars that shine
   And twinkle on the Milky Way,
They stretch'd in never-ending line
   Along the margin of a bay:
Ten thousand saw I at a glance,
Tossing their heads in sprightly dance.

The waves beside them danced, but they
   Out-did the sparkling waves in glee:
A poet could not but be gay,
   In such a jocund company:
I gazed – and gazed – but little thought
What wealth the show to me had brought:

For oft, when on my couch I lie
   In vacant or in pensive mood,
They flash upon that inward eye
   Which is the bliss of solitude;
And then my heart with pleasure fills,
And dances with the daffodils.

William Wordsworth

The Piano

The piano eats with chopsticks
cool minims
diced demi-semiquavers.

When the lid goes down
the piano is inscrutable,
shining with health.

The piano stands politely
until the next meal, silent
for as long as it takes.

Carol Ann Duffy

Early Country Village Morning

Cocks crowing
Hens knowing
later they will cluck
their laying song

Houses stirring
a donkey clip-clopping
the first market bus
comes juggling along

Soon the sun will give a big yawn
and open her eye
pushing the last bit of darkness
out of the sky

Grace Nichols

The Cow

The friendly cow, all red and white,
I love with all my heart:
She gives me cream with all her might,
To eat with apple-tart.

She wanders lowing here and there,
And yet she cannot stray,
All in the pleasant open air,
The pleasant light of day;

And blown by all the winds that pass
And wet with all the showers,
She walks among the meadow grass
And eats the meadow flowers.

Robert Louis Stevenson

Divorce

I did not promise
to stay with you till death us do part, or
anything like that,
so part I must, and quickly. There are things
I cannot suffer
any longer: Mother, you have never, ever, said
a kind word
or a thank you for all the tedious chores I have done;
Father, your breath
smells like a camel's and gives me the hump;
all you ever say is:
'Are you off in the cream puff, Lady Muck?'
In this day and age?
I would be better off in an orphanage.

I want a divorce.
There are parents in the world whose faces turn
up to the light
who speak in a soft murmur of rivers
and never shout.
There are parents who stroke their children's cheeks
in the dead night
and sing in the colourful voices of rainbows,
red to blue.
These parents are not you. I never chose you.
You are rough and wild,
I don't want to be your child. All you do is shout
and that's not right.
I will file for divorce in the morning at first light.

Jackie Kay

April Rain Song

Let the rain kiss you.
Let the rain beat upon your head with silver liquid drops.
Let the rain sing you a lullaby.

The rain makes still pools on the sidewalk.
The rain makes running pools in the gutter.
The rain plays a little sleep-song on our roof at night –

And I love the rain.

Langston Hughes

New Sights

I like to see a thing I know
Has not been seen before,
That's why I cut my apple through
To look into the core.

It's nice to think, though many an eye
Has seen the ruddy skin,
Mine is the very first to spy
The five brown pips within.

Anon.

Poetman

The Poetman
calls at each house
in the early hours.

When the stars are frosted flowers
and the night a velvet mole.

The Poetman shoulders his bundle –

at each doorstep
he sheds a poem or two.

He whistles surprises in the dark.
Like a waking spell.

Dogs bark back a greeting.
Cats arch and purr.

In bedrooms children stir.
The moon grins

a thin-lipped smile.
Sleepy poems like fragile reptiles

slither indoors.
Still curled in our beds

our dreamy heads catch
the sound of their snores.

Pie Corbett

Maggie

There was a small maiden named Maggie,
Whose dog was enormous and shaggy;
The front end of him
Looked vicious and grim –
But the tail end was friendly and waggy.

Anon.

My Sari

Saris hang on the washing line:
a rainbow in our neighbourhood.
This little orange one is mine,
it has a mango leaf design.
I wear it as a Rani would.
It wraps round me like sunshine,
it ripples silky down my spine,
and I stand tall and feel so good.

Debjani Chatterjee

Little Trotty Wagtail

Little trotty wagtail, he went in the rain,
And tittering, tottering sideways he ne'er got straight again.
He stooped to get a worm, and look'd up to catch a fly,
And then he flew away ere his feathers they were dry.

Little trotty wagtail, he waddled in the mud,
And left his little footmarks, trample where he would.
He waddled in the water-pudge, and waggle went his tail,
And he chirrup up his wings to dry upon the garden rail.

Little trotty wagtail, you nimble all about,
And in the dimpling water-pudge you waddle in and out;
Your home is nigh at hand, and in the warm pigsty,
So, little Master Wagtail, I'll bid you a goodbye.

John Clare

Home Thoughts from Abroad

Oh, to be in England
Now that April's there,
And whoever wakes in England
Sees, some morning, unaware,
That the lowest boughs and the brushwood sheaf
Round the elm-tree bole are in tiny leaf,
While the chaffinch sings on the orchard bough
In England – now!
And after April, when May follows,
And the whitethroat builds, and all the swallows!
Hark, where my blossomed pear-tree in the hedge
Leans to the field and scatters on the clover
Blossoms and dewdrops – at the bent spray's edge –
That's the wise thrush; he sings each song twice over,
Lest you should think he never could recapture
The first fine careless rapture!
And though the fields look rough with hoary dew,
All will be gay when noontide wakes anew
The buttercups, the little children's dower
– Far brighter than this gaudy melon-flower.

Robert Browning

SS Titanic
15 April 1912

First there was silence. Not below,
where silver forks and laughter
chink in each saloon;
where layered decks of dance and song
echo through perfumed corridors,
all set to last till dawn.
Nor several tiers down
in simpler quarters.
There, for the first time ocean-borne,
emigrants still chatter,
more subdued in tone;
entrust to some far-off new world
their dreams
and all they own.

But high above the deck
is peace.
The wind is slight,
though the air has chilled surprisingly:
little swell,
no waves to speak of,
movement smooth, unhampered.
The theatre set.
Viewed from the gods her course is clear,
pulled, as if by chains, on steady track
towards her destination.
Behind, the wake spreads endlessly,
stretches wide then slowly fades
into the night.

Only a faint jarring interrupts
that almost total silence of the sea,
barely noticed by the revellers.
There is no panic.
A brief encounter with an icy shelf
means nothing to a ship that is
unsinkable . . .

Later, she begins to list;
the rest is known.
Emigrants from flooded cabins
claw through dark companionways,
held back to save the rich;
lifeboats lowered quarter-full;
the shameless fights for precedence.

And for the rest,
gathering in disbelief on darkened decks,
the wait.
One weeps,
one lights a cigarette,
one goes below, changes to evening dress
to meet his fate.
On sloping decks the band play on –
Hold me up in high waters
their almost final line.

At last, she rises almost vertical –
a lifelong memory
for those who lived to tell the tale –
then slides, nose-first
towards her brave new world
encompassed only by
the lasting silence of the sea,
the silence of the sky.

Judith Nicholls

In Mrs Tilscher's Class

You could travel up the Blue Nile
with your finger, tracing the route
while Mrs Tilscher chanted the scenery.
Tana. Ethiopia. Khartoum. Aswan.
That for an hour, then a skittle of milk
and the chalky Pyramids rubbed into dust.
A window opened with a long pole.
The laugh of a bell swung by a running child.

This was better than home. Enthralling books.
The classroom glowed like a sweet shop.
Sugar paper. Coloured shapes. Brady and Hindley
faded, like the faint, uneasy smudge of a mistake.
Mrs Tilscher loved you. Some mornings, you found
she'd left a good gold star by your name.
The scent of a pencil slowly, carefully, shaved.
A xylophone's nonsense heard from another form.

April

Over the Easter term, the inky tadpoles changed
from commas into exclamation marks. Three frogs
hopped in the playground, freed by a dunce,
followed by a line of kids, jumping and croaking
away from the lunch queue. A rough boy
told you how you were born. You kicked him, but stared
at your parents, appalled, when you got back home.

The feverish July, the air tasted of electricity.
A tangible alarm made you always untidy, hot,
fractious under the heavy, sexy sky. You asked her
how you were born and Mrs Tilscher smiled,
then turned away. Reports were handed out.
You ran through the gates, impatient to be grown,
as the sky split open into a thunderstorm.

Carol Ann Duffy

The Cuckoo

O the cuckoo she's a pretty bird,
   She singeth as she flies,
She bringeth good tidings,
   She telleth no lies.

She sucketh white flowers,
   For to keep her voice clear,
And the more she singeth cuckoo,
   The summer draweth near.

Anon.

A Song of Toad

The world has held great Heroes,
   As history-books have showed;
But never a name to go down to fame
   Compared to that of Toad!

The clever men at Oxford
   Know all that there is to be knowed.
But they none of them know one half as much
   As intelligent Mr Toad!

The animals sat in the ark and cried,
   Their tears in torrents flowed.
Who was it said, 'There's land ahead'?
   Encouraging Mr Toad!

The Army all saluted
   As they marched along the road.
Was it the King? Or Kitchener?
   No. It was Mr Toad.

The Queen and her ladies-in-waiting
   Sat at the window and sewed.
She cried, 'Look! Who's that *handsome* man?'
   They answered, 'Mr Toad.'

The motor-car went Poop-poop-poop
   As it raced along the road.
Who was it steered it into a pond?
   Ingenious Mr Toad!

Kenneth Grahame

Cat

Sometimes I am an unseen
marmalade cat, the friendliest colour,
making off through a window without permission,
pacing along a broken-glass wall to the greenhouse
jumping down with a soft, four-pawed thump,
finding two inches open of the creaking door
with the loose brass handle,
slipping impossibly in,
flattening my fur at the hush and touch of the sudden warm
      air,
avoiding the tiled gutter of slow green water,
skirting the potted nests of tetchy cactuses,
and sitting with my tail flicked
skilfully underneath me, to sniff
the azaleas   the azaleas   the azaleas.

Alan Brownjohn

The Owl and the Astronaut

The owl and the astronaut
Sailed through space
In their intergalactic ship
They kept hunger at bay
With three pills a day
And drank through a protein drip.
The owl dreamed of mince
And slices of quince
And remarked how life had gone flat;
'It may be all right
To fly faster than light
But I preferred the boat and the cat.'

Gareth Owen

Morning

Morning comes
    with a milk-float jiggling

Morning comes
    with a milkman whistling

Morning comes
    with empties clinking

Morning comes
    with alarm-clock ringing

Morning comes
    with toaster popping

Morning comes
    with letters dropping

Morning comes
    with kettle singing

Morning comes
    with me just listening

Morning comes to drag me out of bed
— Boss-Woman Morning.

Grace Nichols

Cats

Cats are contradictions; tooth and claw
Velvet-padded;
Snowflake-gentle paw
A fist of pins;
Kettles on the purr
Ready to spit;
Black silk, then bristled fur.

Cats are of the East –
Scimitar and sphinx;
Sunlight striped with shade.
Leopard, lion, lynx
Moss-footed in a frightened glade;
Slit eyes an amber glint
Of boring through the darkness cool as jade.

Cats have come to rest
Upon the cushioned West,
Here, dyed-in-the-silk,
They lap up bottled milk –
And that of human kindness –
And return
To the mottled woods of Spring
Making the trees afraid
With leaf and wing
A-flutter at the movement of the fern.

Midnight-wild
With phosphorescent eyes,
Cats are morning-wise
Sleeping as they stare into the sun,
Blind to the light,
Deaf to echoing cries,
From a ravaged wood
Cats see black and white,
Morning and night as one.

Phoebe Hesketh

Magpies

One for sorrow, two for joy,
Three for a kiss and four for a boy,
Five for silver, six for gold,
Seven for a secret never to be told,
Eight for a letter over the sea,
Nine for a lover as true as can be.

Anon.

Billy McBone

Billy McBone
Had a mind of his own,
Which he mostly kept under his hat.
The teachers all thought
That he couldn't be taught,
But Bill didn't seem to mind that.

Billy McBone
Had a mind of his own,
Which the teachers had searched for for years.
Trying test after test,
They still never guessed
It was hidden between his ears.

Billy McBone,
Had a mind of his own,
Which only his friends ever saw.
When the teacher said, 'Bill,
Whereabouts is Brazil?'
He just shuffled and stared at the floor.

Billy McBone
Had a mind of his own,
Which he kept under lock and key.
While the teachers in vain
Tried to burgle his brain,
Bill's thoughts were off wandering free.

Allan Ahlberg

Cow

The Cow comes home swinging
Her udder and singing:

'The dirt O the dirt
It does me no hurt.

And a good splash of muck
Is a blessing of luck.

O I splosh through the mud
But the breath of my cud

Is sweeter than silk.
O I splush through manure

But my heart stays pure
As a pitcher of milk.'

Ted Hughes

I'd Love to be a Fairy's Child

Children born of fairy stock
Never need for shirt or frock,
Never want for food or fire,
Always get their heart's desire:
Jingle pockets full of gold,
Marry when they're seven years old,
Every fairy child may keep
Two strong ponies and ten sheep;
All have houses, each his own,
Built of brick or granite stone;
They live on cherries, they run wild –
I'd love to be a fairy's child.

Robert Graves

Fish

fat
cat
swish
fish

purr
fur
wish
fish

paw
below
dip
flip

mouth
wide
fish
slip
slide
inside

lips
lick

cat
nap

John Cunliffe

All the Dogs

You should have seen him –
he stood in the park and whistled,
underneath an oak tree,
and all the dogs came bounding up
and sat around him,
keeping their big eyes on him,
tails going like pendulums.
And there was one cocker pup
who went and licked his hand,
and a Labrador who whimpered
till the rest joined in.

Then he whistled a second time,
high-pitched as a stoat,
over all the shouted dog names
and whistles of owners,
till a flurry of paws
brought more dogs, panting,
as if they'd come miles,
and these too found space
on the flattened grass
to stare at the boy's
unmemorable face
which all the dogs found special.

Matthew Sweeney

Coolscorin'Matchwinnin' Celebratin'Striker!

I'm a shirt removin' crowd salutin'
handstandin' happy landin'
rockin' rollin' divin' slidin'
posin' poutin' loud shoutin'
pistol packin' smoke blowin'
flag wavin' kiss throwin'
hipswingin' armwavin'
breakdancin' cool ravin'
shoulder shruggin' team huggin'
hot shootin' rootin' tootin'
somersaultin' fence vaultin'
last minute goal grinnin'
shimmy shootin' shin spinnin'
celebratin' cup winnin' STRIKER!

Paul Cookson

The Tyger

Tyger! Tyger! burning bright
In the forests of the night,
What immortal hand or eye
Could frame thy fearful symmetry?

In what distant deeps or skies
Burnt the fire of thine eyes?
On what wings dare he aspire?
What the hand dare seize the fire?

And what shoulder, and what art,
Could twist the sinews of thy heart?
And when thy heart began to beat,
What dread hand? and what dread feet?

What the hammer? what the chain?
In what furnace was thy brain?
What the anvil? what dread grasp
Dare its deadly terrors clasp?

When the stars threw down their spears,
And water'd heaven with their tears,
Did he smile his work to see?
Did he who made the Lamb make thee?

Tyger! Tyger! burning bright
In the forests of the night,
What immortal hand or eye
Dare frame thy fearful symmetry?

William Blake

May

Futility

Move him into the sun –
Gently its touch awoke him once,
At home, whispering of fields unsown.
Always it woke him, even in France,
Until this morning and this snow.
If anything might rouse him now
The kind old sun will know.

Think how it wakes the seeds, –
Woke, once, the clays of a cold star.
Are limbs so dear-achieved, are sides,
Full-nerved, – still warm, – too hard to stir?
Was it for this the clay grew tall?
– O what made fatuous sunbeams toil
To break earth's sleep at all?

Wilfred Owen

Hippopotamus

The hippopotamus –
how odd –
loves rolling
in the river mud.

It makes him
neither hale nor ruddy,
just lovely
hippopotamuddy.

N.M. Bodecker

We Are Going to See the Rabbit

We are going to see the rabbit,
We are going to see the rabbit.
Which rabbit, people say?
Which rabbit, ask the children?
Which rabbit?
The only rabbit,
The only rabbit in England,
Sitting behind a barbed-wire fence
Under the floodlights, neon lights,
Sodium lights,
Nibbling grass
On the only patch of grass
In England, in England
(Except the grass by the hoardings
Which doesn't count.)
We are going to see the rabbit
And we must be there on time.

First we shall go by escalator,
Then we shall go by underground,
And then we shall go by motorway
And then by helicopterway,
And the last ten yards we shall have to go
On foot.

And now we are going
All the way to see the rabbit.
We are nearly there,
We are longing to see it,
And so is the crowd
Which is here in thousands
With mounted policemen
And big loudspeakers
And bands and banners,
And everyone has come a long way.
But soon we shall see it
Sitting and nibbling
The blades of grass
On the only patch of grass
In – but something has gone wrong!
Why is everyone so angry,
Why is everyone jostling
And slanging and complaining?

The rabbit has gone,
Yes, the rabbit has gone.
He has actually burrowed down into the earth
And made himself a warren, under the earth,
Despite all these people.
And what shall we do?
What *can* we do?

It is all a pity, you must be disappointed,
Go home and do something else for today,
Go home again, go home for today.
For you cannot hear the rabbit, under the earth,
Remarking rather sadly to himself, by himself,
As he rests in his warren, under the earth:
'It won't be long, they are bound to come,
They are bound to come and find me, even here.'

Alan Brownjohn

The Owl and the Pussy-Cat

The Owl and the Pussy-Cat went to sea
    In a beautiful pea-green boat,
They took some honey, and plenty of money,
    Wrapped up in a five-pound note.
The Owl looked up to the stars above,
    And sang to a small guitar,
'O lovely Pussy! O Pussy, my love,
        What a beautiful Pussy you are,
            You are,
            You are!
        What a beautiful Pussy you are!'

Pussy said to the Owl, 'You elegant fowl!
    How charmingly sweet you sing!
O let us be married! too long have we tarried:
    But what shall we do for a ring?'
They sailed away, for a year and a day,
    To the land where the Bong-tree grows,
And there in a wood a Piggy-wig stood
        With a ring at the end of his nose,
            His nose,
            His nose,
        With a ring at the end of his nose.

'Dear Pig, are you willing to sell for one shilling
   Your ring?' Said the Piggy, 'I will.'
So they took it away, and were married next day
   By the Turkey who lives on the hill.
They dined on mince, and slices of quince,
   Which they ate with a runcible spoon;
And hand in hand, on the edge of the sand,
     They danced by the light of the moon,
      The moon,
      The moon,
     They danced by the light of the moon.

Edward Lear

Bump!

Things that go 'bump!' in the night,
Should not really give one a fright.
It's the hole in each ear
That lets in the fear,
That, and the absence of light!

Spike Milligan

Girl with a Worksheet in a Castle

There's a castle we visit where Mr Barret talks
　battlements, baileys and barbicans.

But when I've done my worksheet and my sketches,
　down unsafe stairs I find this lonely place,

this earth-floored larder. I breathe deeply in
　the stink of centuries. An ancient chef

sweats. Humps sacks of onions, spuds,
　turnips and garlic. Thinks of wine and oil

he'll baste over mutton, pork or fish. I hear
　salt Saxon shouts. Alone, I'm history

and history is me. But still . . . be still . . .
　　　　　　　　　　　　　　　　Then
　Mr Barret's calling *Eleanor Smith*!

He asks me about battlements and baileys,
　and, not this lonely place, this worksheet.

　　　　　　　　　　　　　　　Fred Sedgwick

Upon Westminster Bridge

Earth has not anything to show more fair:
Dull would he be of soul who could pass by
A sight so touching in its majesty:
This City now doth, like a garment, wear
The beauty of the morning; silent, bare,
Ships, towers, domes, theatres, and temples lie
Open unto the fields, and to the sky;
All bright and glittering in the smokeless air.
Never did sun more beautifully steep
In his first splendour, valley, rock, or hill;
Ne'er saw I, never felt, a calm so deep!
The river glideth at his own sweet will:
Dear God! the very houses seem asleep;
And all the mighty heart is lying still!

William Wordsworth

The Island

They mowed the meadow down below
Our house the other day
But left a grassy island where
We still can go and play.

Right in the middle of the field
It rises green and high;
Bees swing on the clover there,
And butterflies blow by.

It seems a very far-off place
With oceans all around:
The only thing to see is sky,
And wind, the only sound.

Dorothy Aldis

Sea-Fever

I must go down to the seas again, to the lonely sea and the
   sky,
And all I ask is a tall ship and a star to steer her by,
And the wheel's kick and the wind's song and the white
   sail's shaking,
And a grey mist on the sea's face and a grey dawn breaking.

I must go down to the seas again, for the call of the running
   tide
Is a wild call and a clear call that may not be denied;
And all I ask is a windy day with the white clouds flying,
And the flung spray and the blown spume, and the sea-gulls
   crying.

I must go down to the seas again, to the vagrant gypsy life,
To the gull's way and the whale's way where the wind's like
   a whetted knife;
And all I ask is a merry yarn from a laughing fellow-rover,
And quiet sleep and a sweet dream when the long trick's
   over.

John Masefield

Cows

Half the time they munched the grass, and all the time they
  lay
Down in the water-meadows, the lazy month of May,
    A-chewing,
    A-mooing,
  To pass the hours away.

'Nice weather,' said the brown cow,
  'Ah,' said the white.
'Grass is very tasty,'
  'Grass is all right.'

Half the time they munched the grass, and all the time they
  lay
Down in the water-meadows, the lazy month of May,
    A-chewing,
    A-mooing,
  To pass the hours away.

'Rain coming,' said the brown cow,
    'Ah,' said the white.
'Flies is very tiresome.'
    'Flies bite.'

Half the time they munched the grass, and all the time they
    lay
Down in the water-meadows, the lazy month of May,
    A-chewing,
    A-mooing,
    To pass the hours away.

'Time to go,' said the brown cow,
    'Ah,' said the white.
'Nice chat.' 'Very pleasant.'
    'Night.' 'Night.'

Half the time they munched the grass, and all the time they
    lay
Down in the water-meadows, the lazy month of May,
    A-chewing,
    A-mooing,
    To pass the hours away.

James Reeves

Ariel's Song

Full fathom five thy father lies,
    Of his bones are coral made:
Those are pearls that were his eyes,
    Nothing of him that doth fade,
But doth suffer a sea-change
Into something rich, and strange:
Sea-nymphs hourly ring his knell –
    Hark! now I hear them,
      Ding-dong bell.

        William Shakespeare

A Bad Case of Fish

A chip-shop owner's in the dock
on a charge of assault and battery.
The monkfish takes the oath:
So help me cod . . .

The courtroom's packed with lost soles.
The crabby judge can't find his plaice
or read the prosecution's whiting.
And what sort of fish is a saveloy, anyway?

The young skates are getting bored.
They start skateboarding down the aisles.
The scampi scamper to and fro.
The eels are dancing congers.

But the case is cut and dried.
It's all wrapped up. (Just look
in the evening paper.) Next,
the Krayfish twins . . .

Philip Gross

The Pasture

I'm going out to clean the pasture spring;
I'll only stop to rake the leaves away
(And wait to watch the water clear, I may):
I shan't be gone long. – You come too.

I'm going out to fetch the little calf
That's standing by the mother. It's so young
It totters when she licks it with her tongue.
I shan't be gone long. You come too.

Robert Frost

Okay, Brown Girl, Okay

for Josie, 9 years old, who wrote to me saying . . . 'boys called me names because of my colour. I felt very upset . . . My brother and sister are English. I wish I was, then I won't be picked on . . . How do you like being brown?'

Josie, Josie, I am okay
being brown. I remember,
every day dusk and dawn get born
from the loving of night and light
who work together, like married.
     And they would like to say to you:
     Be at school on and on, brown Josie
     like thousands and thousands and thousands
     of children, who are brown and white
     and black and pale-lemon colour.
     All the time, brown girl Josie is okay.

Josie, Josie, I am okay
being brown. I remember,
every minute sun in the sky
and ground of the earth work together
like married.
   And they would like to say to you:
   Ride on up a going escalator
   like thousands and thousands and thousands
   of people, who are brown and white
   and black and pale-lemon colour.
   All the time, brown girl Josie is okay.

Josie, Josie, I am okay
being brown. I remember,
all the time bright-sky and brown-earth
work together, like married
making forests and food and flowers and rain.
   And they would like to say to you:
   Grow and grow and brightly, brown girl.
   Write and read and play and work.
   Ride bus or train or boat or aeroplane
   like thousands and thousands and thousands
   of people, who are brown and white
   and black and pale-lemon colour.
   All the time, brown girl Josie is okay.

James Berry

The Railway Children

When we climbed the slopes of the cutting
We were eye-level with the white cups
Of the telegraph poles and the sizzling wires.

Like lovely freehand they curved for miles
East and miles west beyond us, sagging
Under their burden of swallows.

We were small and thought we knew nothing
Worth knowing. We thought words travelled the wires
In the shiny pouches of raindrops,

Each one seeded full with the light
Of the sky, the gleam of the lines, and ourselves
So infinitesimally scaled

We could stream through the eye of a needle.

Seamus Heaney

Clouds

Have you watched the clouds this year?
Have you noticed the many changes, the diverse colours, the
   drift
And dance and jump and falling away? Have you seen
The gallant scarlet, the gentle pink, the sky
Black and purple and almost green and always
Turning inside out,
Turning and twisting and writhing and seldom still?
But when it is a glory, a feast galore,
It is like the rolling over of foam on the shore,
It is like a mountain-range, the Alps, maybe,
It is what you want to see.
And what you never imagined could be, it is
A glamour, a glory of air, such bold sunsets,
Such risings up in the East. A folding of clouds
Is kind to the eyes, is a painted lullaby.
And there are few words to say why
Colours and ruffs and bubbles and bold balloons
Take our hearts, lift our spirits and glow
In our faster-beating hearts, in our minds also.
We need new words for the sky.

Elizabeth Jennings

Dover Beach

The sea is calm tonight.
The tide is full, the moon lies fair
Upon the straits; – on the French coast the light
Gleams and is gone; the cliffs of England stand,
Glimmering and vast, out in the tranquil bay.
Come to the window, sweet is the night-air!
Only, from the long line of spray
Where the sea meets the moon-blanched land,
Listen! you hear the grating roar
Of pebbles which the waves draw back, and fling,
At their return, up the high strand,
Begin, and cease, and then again begin,
With tremulous cadence slow, and bring
The eternal note of sadness in.

Sophocles long ago
Heard it on the Aegean, and brought
Into his mind the turbid ebb and flow
Of human misery; we
Find also in the sound a thought,
Hearing it by this distant northern sea.

The Sea of Faith
Was once, too, at the full, and round earth's shore
Lay like the folds of a bright girdle furled.
But now I only hear
Its melancholy, long, withdrawing roar,
Retreating, to the breath
Of the night-wind, down the vast edges drear
And naked shingles of the world.

Ah, love, let us be true
To one another! for the world, which seems
To lie before us like a land of dreams,
So various, so beautiful, so new,
Hath really neither joy, nor love, nor light,
Nor certitude, nor peace, nor help for pain;
And we are here as on a darkling plain
Swept with confused alarms of struggle and flight,
Where ignorant armies clash by night.

Matthew Arnold

Here is the Feather WarCast

In the South it will be a dowdy clay
with some shattered scours.
Further North there'll be some hoe and snail
with whales to the Guest.
In the East the roaring pain
will give way to some psalmy bun.

Trevor Millum

Poem for a Country Child

There was a bird and he went hop hop
There was a bird that sang so sweet
It wasn't a robin, a cock or a linnet
It wasn't a cuckoo, a crow or a pigeon
But my own sweet bird.

There was a cow and she went plod plod
There was a cow and she breathed so warm
She wasn't a Friesian, a brindle, a shorthorn
She wasn't a Jersey, piebald, a fierce one
But my own dear cow.

There was a garden and it was mine.
It wasn't a show place, there wasn't a lawn.
There was an old swing and a broken-down fence
And a pile for a bonfire and birds that came hop
Hop hop to my feet if I sat very still
And cows that moved slowly in the green field
My sweet green field.

Jenny Joseph

Adlestrop

Yes. I remember Adlestrop –
The name, because one afternoon
Of heat the express-train drew up there
Unwontedly. It was late June.

The steam hissed. Someone cleared his throat.
No one left and no one came
On the bare platform. What I saw
Was Adlestrop – only the name

And willows, willow-herb, and grass,
And meadowsweet, and haycocks dry,
No whit less still and lonely fair
Than the high cloudlets in the sky.

And for that minute a blackbird sang
Close by, and round him, mistier,
Farther and farther, all the birds
Of Oxfordshire and Gloucestershire.

Edward Thomas

The Rules that Rule the School

Only speak when you're spoken to.
Don't stand and grin like a fool.
Pay attention or risk a detention.
We're the rules that rule the school.

Hands must not be in pockets
When addressing a member of staff.
Though smiling is sometimes permitted,
You need written permission to laugh.

Boys must stand to attention
And salute when they pass the Head.
Girls are expected to curtsey
And lower their eyes instead.

Sit up straight. Do as you're told,
If you want to come top of the class.
Bribes must be paid in cash
If you want to be sure to pass.

Don't breathe too loud in lessons.
Don't sweat too much in games.
Remember that teachers are human.
Don't *ever* call them names.

Only speak when you're spoken to.
Don't stand and grin like a fool.
Pay attention or risk detention.
We're the rules that rule the school.

John Foster

Smelling Rats

My mother said she'd 'smelt a rat',
but none of us knew what she meant.
I wondered what a rat smelt like –
They lived in sewers, Sarah said,
where they grew big as tom cats,
if cornered would go for the throat.
They made brief film appearances,
dancing on Dracula's coffin,
Gangsters muttered, 'you dirty rat',
scientists kept them in cages,
testing lipstick and disease.
They ran on to boats up anchor lines
and of course we all knew
that they carried the plague.
Bubonic plague.
'BEW BON NICK . . .'
We whispered the words
so Mum wouldn't hear,
and sniffed deep
but, smelt nothing.

So we left her to hunt for the rat
and ran down the garden calling,
'Bring out your dead!'
Later that night I lay in bed,
and heard the dread sound
of whatever it was that she sensed.
I lay in the dark
and sniffed . . .

Pie Corbett

And Did Those Feet in Ancient Time

And did those feet in ancient time
Walk upon England's mountains green?
And was the holy lamb of God
On England's pleasant pastures seen?

And did the countenance divine
Shine forth upon our clouded hills?
And was Jerusalem builded here
Among those dark satanic mills?

Bring me my bow of burning gold:
Bring me my arrows of desire:
Bring me my spear: O clouds unfold!
Bring me my chariot of fire.

I will not cease from mental fight,
Nor shall my sword sleep in my hand
Till we have built Jerusalem
In England's green and pleasant land.

William Blake

The World is Day-breaking

The world is day-breaking!
The world is day-breaking!

Day arises
From its sleep.
Day wakes up
With the dawning light.
The world is day-breaking!
The world is day-breaking!

Anon.

If . . .

If ships sailed on the motorway
   and potato crisps were blue,
if football boots were made of silk
   and a lamp-post wore a shoe.

If motorbikes ran upwards
   and milk floats really floated,
if beds were full of dinosaurs
   and peas were sugar-coated.

If flies wore bomber-jackets
   and eggs laid little chickens,
if spacemen had a panther each
   and insects studied Dickens.

If babies' prams were motorized
   and you listened to your conscience,
if your brain was working properly
   you wouldn't read this nonscience.

John Rice

Warning

When I am an old woman I shall wear purple
With a red hat which doesn't go, and doesn't suit me,
And I shall spend my pension on brandy and summer gloves
And satin sandals, and say we've no money for butter.
I shall sit down on the pavement when I'm tired
And gobble up samples in shops and press alarm bells
And run my stick along the public railings
And make up for the sobriety of my youth.
I shall go out in my slippers in the rain
And pick the flowers in other people's gardens
And learn to spit.

You can wear terrible shirts and grow more fat
And eat three pounds of sausages at a go
Or only bread and pickle for a week
And hoard pens and pencils and beermats and things in
   boxes.

But now we must have clothes that keep us dry
And pay the rent and not swear in the street
And set a good example for the children.
We must have friends to dinner and read the papers.

But maybe I ought to practise a little now?
So people who know me are not too shocked and surprised
When suddenly I am old and start to wear purple.

Jenny Joseph

Busy Day

Pop in
pop out
pop over the road
pop out for a walk
pop in for a talk
pop down to the shop
can't stop
got to pop

got to pop?

pop where?
pop what?

well
I've got to
pop round
pop up
pop in to town
pop out to see
pop in for tea
pop down to the shop
can't stop
got to pop

got to pop?

pop where?
pop what?

well
I've got to
pop in
pop out
pop over the road
pop out for a walk
pop in for a talk . . .

Michael Rosen

Lines

I must never daydream in schooltime.
I just love a daydream in Mayshine.
I must ever greydream in timeschool.
Why must others paydream in schoolway?
Just over highschool dismay lay.
Thrust over skydreams in cryschool.
Cry dust over drydreams in screamtime.
Dreamschool thirst first in dismayday.
Why lie for greyday in crimedream?
My time for dreamday is soontime.
In soontime must I daydream ever.
Never must I say dream in strifetime.
Cry dust over daydreams of lifetimes.
I must never daydream in schooltime.
In time I must daydream never.

Judith Nicholls

Chocs

Into the half-pound box of Moonlight
my small hand crept.
There was an electrifying rustle.
There was a dark and glamorous scent.
Into my open, moist mouth
the first Montelimar went.

Down in the crinkly second layer,
five finger-piglets snuffled
among the Hazelnut Whirl,
the Caramel Square,
the Black Cherry and Almond Truffle.

Bliss.

I chomped. I gorged.
I stuffed my face,
till only the Coffee Cream
was left for the owner of the box –
tough luck, Anne Pope –
oh, and half an Orange Supreme.

Carol Ann Duffy

Simple Simon

Simple Simon met a pieman
   Going to the fair;
Says Simple Simon to the pieman,
   'Let me taste your ware.'

Says the pieman unto Simon,
   'Show me first your penny';
Says Simple Simon to the pieman,
   'Indeed I have not any.'

Simple Simon went a-fishing,
   For to catch a whale;
All the water he had got
   Was in his mother's pail.

Simple Simon went to look
   If plums grew on a thistle;
He pricked his fingers very much
   Which made poor Simon whistle.

Anon.

2 Poems about 4 Eyes

They call me Specky Four Eyes.
I wear glasses, so it's true,
I can see quite well why you're teasing me,
I've got two more eyes than you.

My spectacles are magical
for when you taunt and jeer,
I only have to take them off
to make you disappear.

Lindsay MacRae

June

Don't Cry, Caterpillar

Don't cry, Caterpillar
Caterpillar, don't cry
You'll be a butterfly – by and by.

Caterpillar, please
Don't worry 'bout a thing

'But,' said Caterpillar,
'Will I still know myself – in wings?'

Grace Nichols

The Lonely Dragon

A dragon is sad
Because everyone thinks
A dragon is fierce and brave,
And roars out flames,
And eats everybody,
Whoever comes near his cave.
But a dragon likes people,
A dragon needs friends,
A dragon is lonely and sad,
If anyone knows
Of a friend for a dragon,
A dragon would be very glad.

Theresa Heine

Noise

Billy is blowing his trumpet;
Bertie is banging a tin;
Betty is crying for Mummy
And Bob has pricked Ben with a pin.
Baby is crying out loudly;
He's out on the lawn in his pram.
I am the only one silent
And I've eaten all of the jam.

Anon.

Scarborough Fair

Where are you going? To Scarborough Fair?
Parsley, sage, rosemary and thyme,
Remember me to a bonny lass there,
For once she was a true lover of mine.

Tell her to make me a cambric shirt,
Parsley, sage, rosemary and thyme,
Without any needle or thread work'd in it,
And she shall be a true lover of mine.

Tell her to wash it in yonder well,
Parsley, sage, rosemary and thyme,
Where water ne'er sprung nor a drop of rain fell,
And she shall be a true lover of mine.

Tell her to plough me an acre of land,
Parsley, sage, rosemary and thyme,
Between the sea and the salt sea strand,
And she shall be a true lover of mine.

Tell her to plough it with one ram's horn,
Parsley, sage, rosemary and thyme,
And sow it all over with one peppercorn,
And she shall be a true lover of mine.

Tell her to reap it with a sickle of leather,
Parsley, sage, rosemary and thyme,
And tie it all up with a tom tit's feather,
And she shall be a true lover of mine.

Tell her to gather it all in a sack,
Parsley, sage, rosemary and thyme,
And carry it home on a butterfly's back,
And then she shall be a true lover of mine.

Anon.

A Red, Red Rose

O, my Luve's like a red, red rose,
　That's newly sprung in June.
O, my Luve's like the melodie
　That's sweetly play'd in tune.

As fair art thou, my bonnie lass,
　So deep in luve am I;
And I will love thee still, my dear.
　Till a' the seas gang dry.

Till a' the seas gang dry, my dear,
　And the rocks melt wi' the sun:
I will love thee still, my dear,
　While the sands o' life shall run:

And fare thee weel, my only luve!
　And fare thee weel, a while!
And I will come again, my luve,
　Tho' it ware ten thousand mile!

Robert Burns

194

Gust Becos I Cud Not Spel

Gust becos I cud not spel
It did not mean I was daft
When the boys in school red my riting
Some of them laffed.

But now I am the dictater
They have to rite like me
Utherwise they cannot pas
Ther GCSE

Some of the girls wer ok
But those who laffed a lot
Have al bean rownded up
And hav recintly bean shot

The teecher who corrected my speling
As not been shot at al
But four the last fifteen howers
As bean standing up against a wal

He has to stand ther until he can spel
Figgymisgrugifooniyn the rite way
I think he will stand ther forever
I just inventid it today

Brian Patten

Madame Mouse

Madame Mouse trots,
Grey in the black night!
Madame Mouse trots:
Furred is the light.
The elephant-trunks
Trumpet from the sea . . .
Grey in the black night
The mouse trots free.
Hoarse as a dog's bark
The heavy leaves are furled . . .
The cat's in his cradle,
All's well with the world!

Edith Sitwell

When I Was a Hundred and Twenty-Six

When I was a hundred and twenty-six
And you were a hundred and four
What fun, my dearest dear, we had
At the back of the Co-op store.
It was all such a very long time ago
That it seems just like a dream
In the days when you called me your own Rich Tea
And you were my Custard Cream.

Such joys we knew with those dinners *à deux*
At the bottom of the parking lot
On roasted gnu and buffalo stew
And Tandoori chicken in a pot.
Such songs, my love, we used to sing
Till the stars had lost their shine,
And the bells of heaven rang ding, ding, ding
And the neighbours rang 999.

When I was a hundred and twenty-six
And you were a hundred and four
We thought love's cherry would last a very
Long time, and then some more.
But days are fleet when ways are sweet
As the honey in the hive –
And I am a hundred and twenty-seven
And you are a hundred and five.

Charles Causley

What Does it Matter?

What does it matter to you and me
Whether it's half past eight or three?
The nursery clock has just gone one;
And hark, the clock in the hall's begun!
But it must be wrong, for it's striking seven;
And there goes another one, on to eleven!
    And I think it's four,
     But it might be more –
Oh, what does it matter to you and me?
Let's have dinner and call it tea!
And we'll all go to bed and wake at three,
   For the Sun will be right in the morning.

E.V. Rieu

The Prayer of the Cat

Lord,
I am a cat,
It is not, exactly, that I have something to ask of You!
No –
I ask nothing of anyone –
but,
if You have by some chance, in some celestial barn,
a little white mouse,
or a saucer of milk,
I know someone who would relish them.
Wouldn't You like some day
to put a curse on the whole race of dogs?
If so I should say,

Amen

Carmen Bernos de Gasztold,
translated from the French by Rumer Godden

The Lamb

Little Lamb, who made thee?
  Dost thou know who made thee?
Gave thee life, and bid thee feed
By the stream and o'er the mead;
Gave thee clothing of delight,
Softest clothing, woolly, bright;
Gave thee such a tender voice,
Making all the vales rejoice?
  Little Lamb, who made thee?
  Dost thou know who made thee?

  Little Lamb, I'll tell thee,
  Little Lamb, I'll tell thee:
He is callèd by thy name,
For He calls himself a Lamb.
He is meek, and He is mild;
He became a little child.
I, a child, and thou a lamb,
We are callèd by His name.
  Little Lamb, God bless thee!
  Little Lamb, God bless thee!

William Blake

Old Noah's Ark

Old Noah once he built an ark,
And patched it up with hickory bark.
He anchored it to a great big rock,
And then he began to load his stock.
The animals went in one by one,
The elephant chewing a carroway bun.
The animals went in two by two,
The crocodile and the kangaroo.
The animals went in three by three,
The tall giraffe and the tiny flea.
The animals went in four by four,
The hippopotamus stuck in the door.
The animals went in five by five,
The bees mistook the bear for a hive.
The animals went in six by six,
The monkey was up to his usual tricks.
The animals went in seven by seven,
Said the ant to the elephant, 'Who're ye shov'n?'
The animals went in eight by eight,
Some were early and some were late.
The animals went in nine by nine,
They all formed fours and marched in line.
The animals went in ten by ten,
If you want any more, you can read it again.

Anon.

Sonnet 18

Shall I compare thee to a summer's day?
Thou art more lovely and more temperate:
Rough winds do shake the darling buds of May,
And summer's lease hath all too short a date:
Sometime too hot the eye of heaven shines,
And often is his gold complexion dimm'd;
And every fair from fair sometime declines,
By chance or nature's changing course untrimm'd;
But thy eternal summer shall not fade,
Nor lose possession of that fair thou ow'st;
Nor shall Death brag thou wander'st in his shade,
When in eternal lines to time thou grow'st:
    So long as men can breathe, or eyes can see,
    So long lives this, and this gives life to thee.

William Shakespeare

Where Do All the Teachers Go?

Where do all the teachers go
When it's four o'clock?
Do they live in houses
And do they wash their socks?

Do they wear pyjamas
And do they watch TV?
And do they pick their noses
The same as you and me?

Do they live with other people
Have they mums and dads?
And were they ever children
And were they ever bad?

Did they ever, never spell right
Did they ever make mistakes?
Were they punished in the corner
If they pinched the chocolate flakes?

Did they ever lose their hymn books
Did they ever leave their greens?
Did they scribble on the desk tops
Did they wear old dirty jeans?

I'll follow one back home today
I'll find out what they do
Then I'll put it in a poem
That they can read to you.

Peter Dixon

Cows on the Beach

Two cows,
fed-up with grass, field, farmer,
barged through barbed wire
and found the beach.
Each mooed to each:
This is a better place to be,
a stretch of sand next to the sea,
this is the place for me.
And they stayed there all day,

strayed this way, that way,
over to rocks,
past discarded socks,
ignoring the few people they met
(it wasn't high season yet).
They dipped hooves in the sea,
got wet up to the knee,
they swallowed pebbles and sand,
found them a bit bland,
washed them down with sea-water,
decided they really ought to
rest for an hour.
Both were sure
they'd never leave here.
Imagine, they'd lived so near
and never knew!
With a swapped moo
they sank into sleep,
woke to the yellow jeep
of the farmer
revving there
feet from the incoming sea.
This is no place for cows to be,
he shouted, and slapped them
with seaweed, all the way home.

Matthew Sweeney

My Pretty Maid

'Where are you going to, my Pretty Maid?'
'I'm going a-milking, Sir,' she said.

'Shall I go with you, my Pretty Maid?'
'Oh yes, if you please, kind Sir,' she said.

'What is your Father, my Pretty Maid?'
'My Father's a Farmer, Sir,' she said.

'Shall I marry you, my Pretty Maid?'
'Oh thank you kindly, Sir,' she said.

'But what is your Fortune, my Pretty Maid?'
'My face is my Fortune, Sir,' she said.

'Then I can't marry you, my Pretty Maid!'
'Nobody asked you, Sir!' she said.

'Nobody asked you, Sir!' she said.

'Sir!' she said.

Anon.

Stickleback

The Stickleback's a spiky chap,
　Worse than a bit of briar.
Hungry Pike would sooner swallow
　Embers from a fire.

The Stickleback is fearless in
　The way he loves his wife.
Every minute of the day
　He guards her with his life.

She, like him, is dressed to kill
　In stiff and steely prickles,
And when they kiss, there bubbles up
　The laughter of the tickles.

Ted Hughes

Walking the Dog Seems Like Fun to Me

I said, The dog wants a walk.

Mum said to Dad, It's your turn.
Dad said, I always walk the dog.
Mum said, Well I walked her this morning.
Dad said, She's your dog.
I didn't want a dog in the first place.

Mum said, It's your turn.

Dad stood up and threw the remote control
at the pot plant.
Dad said, I'm going down the pub.
Mum said, Take the dog.

Dad shouted, No way!
Mum shouted, You're going nowhere!

I grabbed Judy's lead
and we both bolted out the back door.

The stars were shining like diamonds.
Judy sniffed at a hedgehog, rolled up in a ball.
She ate a discarded kebab on the pavement.
She tried to chase a cat that ran up a tree.

Walking the dog
seems like fun to me.

Roger Stevens

The Passionate Shepherd to His Love

Come live with me and be my Love,
And we will all the pleasures prove
That valleys, groves, hills, and fields,
Woods, or steepy mountains yields.

And we will sit upon the rocks
Seeing the shepherds feed their flocks,
By shallow rivers, to whose falls
Melodious birds sing madrigals.

And I will make thee beds of roses
And a thousand fragrant posies,
A cap of flowers, and a kirtle
Embroidered all with leaves of myrtle;

A gown made of the finest wool,
Which from our pretty lambs we pull;
Fair linèd slippers for the cold,
With buckles of the purest gold;

A belt of straw and ivy buds
With coral clasps and amber studs;
And if these pleasures may thee move,
Come live with me and be my Love.

The shepherd swains shall dance and sing
For thy delight each May morning:
If these delights thy mind may move,
Then live with me and be my Love.

Christopher Marlowe

Overheard on a Saltmarsh

Nymph, nymph, what are your beads?

Green glass, goblin. Why do you stare at them?

Give them me.

        No.

Give them me. Give them me.

                No.

Then I will howl all night in the reeds,
Lie in the mud and howl for them.

Goblin, why do you love them so?

They are better than stars or water,
Better than voices of winds that sing,
Better than any man's fair daughter,
Your green glass beads on a silver ring.

Hush, I stole them out of the moon.

Give me your beads. I want them.

                            No.

I will howl in a deep lagoon
For your green glass beads, I love them so.
Give them me. Give them.

                    No.

                    Harold Monro

The Meadow in Midsummer

Immobilized by June heat
the chestnut trees are calm cathedrals
   of bough and leaf.
In their deep shade
half-hidden horses
   seek cool relief.

The pond's azure eye
gazes amazed at the gold coin
    dazzling the sky
as, barefoot amidst buttercups,
we cross the meadow,
    slowly pass by.

Wes Magee

Who would true valour see

Who would true valour see,
Let him come hither;
One here will constant be,
Come wind, come weather.
There's no discouragement
Shall make him once relent
His first avow'd intent,
To be a pilgrim.

Whoso beset him round
With dismal stories,
Do but themselves confound,
His strength the more is.
No lion can him fright,
He'll with a giant fight,
But he will have a right
To be a pilgrim.

Hobgoblin, nor foul fiend,
Can daunt his spirit;
He knows he at the end
Shall life inherit.
Then fancies fly away,
He'll fear not what men say,
He'll labour night and day
To be a pilgrim.

John Bunyan

No Peas for the Wicked

No peas for the wicked
No carrots for the damned
No parsnips for the naughty
  O Lord we pray

No sprouts for the shameless
No cabbage for the shady
No lettuce for the lecherous
  No way, no way

No potatoes for the deviants
No radish for the riff-raff
No spinach for the spineless
  Lock them away

No beetroot for the boasters
No mange-tout for the mobsters
No corn-on-the-cob et cetera
  (Shall we call it a day?)

Roger McGough

Moonlight, Summer Moonlight

'Tis moonlight, summer moonlight,
All soft and still and fair;
The silent time of midnight
Shines sweetly everywhere,

But most where trees are sending
Their breezy boughs on high,
Or stooping low are lending
A shelter from the sky.

Emily Brontë

Hurt No Living Thing

Hurt no living thing,
Ladybird nor butterfly,
Nor moth with dusty wing,
Nor cricket chirping cheerily,
Nor grasshopper, so light of leap,
Nor dancing gnat,
Nor beetle fat,
Nor harmless worms that creep.

Christina Rossetti

Gran Can You Rap?

Gran was in her chair she was taking a nap
When I tapped her on the shoulder to see if she could rap.
Gran can you rap? Can you rap? Can you Gran?
And she opened one eye and said to me, Man,
   I'm the best rapping Gran this world's ever seen
   I'm a tip-top, slip-slap, rap-rap queen.

And she rose from her chair in the corner of the room
And she started to rap with a bim-bam-boom,
And she rolled up her eyes and she rolled round her head
And as she rolled by this is what she said.
   I'm the best rapping Gran this world's ever seen
   I'm a nip-nap, yip-yap, rap-rap queen.

Then she rapped past my dad and she rapped past my
   mother,
She rapped past me and my little baby brother,
She rapped her arms narrow she rapped her arms wide,
She rapped through the door and she rapped outside.
   She's the best rapping Gran this world's ever seen
   She's a drip-drop, trip-trap, rap-rap queen.

She rapped down the garden she rapped down the street,
The neighbours all cheered and they tapped their feet.
She rapped through the traffic lights as they turned red
As she rapped round the corner this is what she said,
　I'm the best rapping Gran this world's ever seen
　I'm a flip-flop, hip-hop, rap-rap queen.

She rapped down the lane she rapped up the hill,
And as she disappeared she was rapping still.
I could hear Gran's voice saying, Listen man,
Listen to the rapping of the rap-rap Gran.
　I'm the best rapping Gran this world's ever seen
　I'm a –
　　　tip-top, slip-slap,
　　　　nip-nap, yip-yap,
　　　　　hip-hop, trip-trap,
　　　　　　touch yer cap,
　　　　　　take a nap,
　　　　　　　happy, happy, happy, happy,
　　　　　　　rap-rap-queen.

Jack Ousbey

Lone Mission

On evenings, after cocoa
(blackout down and sealed)
I would build plasticine Hamburgs
on green lino
and bomb them with encyclopedias
(dropped from ceiling level)
from my Lancaster Bomber
built
(usually)
from table, box and curtains
turret made of chairs
radio and gas masks
tray and kitchen ware
But:
Aircrew were my problem
gunners mid and rear
radio and bomber
nav and engineer.

Each night I flew lone missions
through flak both hot and wild
and learnt it wasn't easy
to be an only child.

Peter Dixon

28

The Rain

The rain has silver sandals
For dancing in the spring,
And shoes with golden tassels
For summer's frolicking.
Her winter boots have hobnails
Of ice from heel to toe,
Which now and then she changes
For moccasins of snow.

May Justus

At the End of a School Day

It is the end of a school day
and down the long drive
come bag-swinging, shouting children.
Deafened, the sky winces.
The sun gapes in surprise.

Suddenly the runners skid to a stop,
stand still and stare
at a small hedgehog
curled up on the tarmac
like an old, frayed cricket ball.

A girl dumps her bag, tiptoes forward
and gingerly, so gingerly
carries the creature
to the safety of a shady hedge.
Then steps back, watching.

Girl, children, sky and sun
hold their breath.
There is silence,
a moment to remember
on this warm afternoon in June.

Wes Magee

The Cow

The cow is of the bovine ilk;
One end is moo, the other, milk.

Ogden Nash

July

The Duel

The gingham dog and the calico cat
Side by side on the table sat;
'Twas half-past twelve, and (what do you think!)
Nor one nor t' other had slept a wink!
  The old Dutch clock and the Chinese plate
  Appeared to know as sure as fate
There was going to be a terrible spat.

  (*I wasn't there; I simply state*
  What was told to me by the Chinese plate!)

The gingham dog went 'bow-wow-wow!'
And the calico cat replied 'mee-ow!'
The air was littered, an hour or so,
With bits of gingham and calico,
  While the old Dutch clock in the chimney-place
  Up with its hands before its face,
For it always dreaded a family row!

July

(Now mind: I'm only telling you
What the old Dutch clock declares is true!)

The Chinese plate looked very blue,
And wailed, 'Oh, dear! what shall we do!'
But the gingham dog and the calico cat
Wallowed this way and tumbled that,
   Employing every tooth and claw
   In the awfullest way you ever saw –
And, oh! how the gingham and calico flew!

(Don't fancy I exaggerate –
I got my news from the Chinese plate!)

Next morning, where the two had sat
They found no trace of dog or cat;
And some folks think unto this day
That burglars stole that pair away!
   But the truth about the cat and pup
   Is this: they ate each other up!
Now what do you really think of that!

(The old Dutch clock it told me so,
And that is how I came to know.)

Eugene Field

maggie and milly and molly and may

maggie and milly and molly and may
went down to the beach(to play one day)

and maggie discovered a shell that sang
so sweetly she couldn't remember her troubles,and

milly befriended a stranded star
whose rays five languid fingers were;

and molly was chased by a horrible thing
which raced sideways while blowing bubbles:and

may came home with a smooth round stone
as small as a world and as large as alone.

For whatever we lose(like a you or a me)
it's always ourselves we find in the sea

e e cummings

3

Days

What are days for?
Days are where we live.
They come, they wake us
Time and time over.
They are to be happy in:
Where can we live but days?

Ah, solving that question
Brings the priest and the doctor
In their long coats
Running over the fields.

Philip Larkin

To a Black Greyhound

Shining black in the shining light,
  Inky black in the golden sun,
Graceful as the swallow's flight,
  Light as a swallow, wingèd one,
Swift as driven hurricane –
  Double-sinewed stretch and spring,
Muffled thud of flying feet,
  See the black dog galloping,
  Hear his wild foot-beat.

See him lie when the day is dead,
  Black curves curled on the boarded floor.
Sleepy eyes, my sleepy-head –
  Eyes that were aflame before.
Gentle now, they burn no more;
  Gentle now and softly warm,
With the fire that made them bright
  Hidden – as when after storm
  Softly falls the night.

God of speed, who makes the fire –
   God of Peace, who lulls the same –
God who gives the fierce desire,
   Lust for blood as fierce as flame –
God who stands in Pity's name –
   Many may ye be or less,
Ye who rule the earth and sun:
   Gods of strength and gentleness,
   Ye are ever one.

Julian Grenfell

The Caterpillar

Brown and furry
Caterpillar in a hurry,
Take your walk
To the shady leaf, or stalk,
Or what not,
Which may be the chosen spot.
No toad to spy you,
Hovering bird of prey pass by you;
Spin and die,
To live again a butterfly.

Christina Rossetti

6

Mice

I think mice
Are rather nice.

Their tails are long,
Their faces small,
They haven't any
Chins at all.
Their ears are pink,
Their teeth are white,
They run about
The house at night.
They nibble things
They shouldn't touch
And no one seems
To like them much.

But I think mice
Are nice.

Rose Fyleman

Tweedle-dum and Tweedle-dee

Tweedle-dum and Tweedle-dee
Resolved to have a battle
For Tweedle-dum said Tweedle-dee
Had spoiled his nice new rattle.

Just then flew by a monstrous crow
As big as a tar-barrel,
Which frightened both the heroes so
They quite forgot their quarrel.

Anon.

I Wanna be a Star

I wanna be a star.
I wanna go far.
I wanna drive around
in a big red car.
I said yeah yeah yeah
I wanna be a star.

I wanna be a hit.
I wanna be *it*.
I wanna see my name
all brightly lit.
I said yeah yeah yeah
I wanna be a hit.

I wanna be the scene.
I wanna be on screen.
I wanna make the cover
of a magazine.
I said yeah yeah yeah
I wanna be the scene.

I wanna be a star.
I wanna be a star.
But I've only got a job
in a burger bar –
so far . . .

Tony Mitton

Watch Your French

When my mum tipped a panful of red-hot fat
Over her foot, she did quite a little chat,
And I won't tell you what she said
But it wasn't:
'Fancy that!
I must try in future to be far more careful
With this red-hot scalding fat!'

When my dad fell over and landed – splat! –
With a trayful of drinks (he'd tripped over the cat)
I won't tell you what he said
But it wasn't:
'Fancy that!
I must try in the future to be far more careful
To step *round* our splendid cat!'

When Uncle Joe brought me a cowboy hat
Back from the States, the dog stomped it flat,
And I won't tell you what I said
But Mum and Dad yelled:
'STOP THAT!
Where did you learn that appalling language?
Come on. Where?'

'I've no idea,' I said,
'No idea.'

Kit Wright

Where the Bee Sucks

Where the bee sucks, there suck I:
In a cowslip's bell I lie;
There I couch when owls do cry.
On the bat's back I do fly
After summer merrily.
Merrily, merrily shall I live now
Under the blossom that hangs on the bough.

William Shakespeare

I Remember, I Remember

I remember, I remember,
The house where I was born,
The little window where the sun
Came peeping in at morn;
He never came a wink too soon,
Nor brought too long a day,
But now, I often wish the night
Had borne my breath away.

I remember, I remember,
The roses, red and white;
The violets, and the lily-cups,
Those flowers made of light!
The lilacs where the robin built,
And where my brother set
The laburnum on his birthday –
The tree is living yet!

I remember, I remember,
Where I was used to swing;
And thought the air must rush as fresh
To swallows on the wing:
My spirit flew in feathers then,
That is so heavy now,
And summer pools could hardly cool
The fever on my brow!

I remember, I remember,
The fir trees dark and high;
I used to think their slender tops
Were close against the sky:
It was a childish ignorance,
But now 'tis little joy
To know I'm farther off from Heav'n
Than when I was a boy.

Thomas Hood

A Green Cornfield

The earth was green, the sky was blue:
    I saw and heard one sunny morn
A skylark hang between the two,
    A singing speck above the corn;

A stage below, in gay accord,
    White butterflies danced on the wing,
And still the singing skylark soared,
    And silent sank and soared to sing.

The cornfield stretched a tender green
    To right and left beside my walks;
I knew he had a nest unseen
    Somewhere among the million stalks.

And as I paused to hear his song
    While swift the sunny moments slid,
Perhaps his mate sat listening long,
    And listened longer than I did.

Christina Rossetti

Little Fish

The tiny fish enjoy themselves
in the sea.
Quick little splinters of life,
their little lives are fun to them
in the sea.

D.H. Lawrence

Tarantella

Do you remember an Inn,
Miranda?
Do you remember an Inn?
And the tedding and the spreading
Of the straw for a bedding,
And the fleas that tease in the High Pyrenees,
And the wine that tasted of the tar?
And the cheers and the jeers of the young muleteers
(Under the vine of the dark verandah)?
Do you remember an Inn, Miranda,
Do you remember an Inn?
And the cheers and the jeers of the young muleteers
Who hadn't got a penny,
And who weren't paying any,
And the hammer at the doors and the Din?
And the Hip! Hop! Hap!
Of the clap
Of the hands to the twirl and the swirl
Of the girl gone chancing,
Glancing,
Dancing,

Backing and advancing,
Snapping of a clapper to the spin
Out and in –
And the Ting, Tong, Tang of the Guitar
Do you remember an Inn,
Miranda?
Do you remember an Inn?

   Never more;
   Miranda,
   Never more.
   Only the high peaks hoar:
   And Aragon a torrent at the door.
   No sound
   In the walls of the Halls where falls
   The tread
   Of the feet of the dead to the ground
   No sound:
   But the boom
   Of the far Waterfall like Doom.

               Hilaire Belloc

What the Mountains Do

What the mountains do is
roar silent warnings over
huge brown and heather-covered spaces

or fill up valleys with dark green laughter

before resting their stone-cropped heads
in sunlight.

David Harmer

Argus and Ulysses

Argus was a puppy,
Frisking full of joy.
Ulysses was his master,
Who sailed away to Troy

Argus on the sea-shore
Watched the ship's white track,
And barked a little puppy-bark
To bring his master back.

Argus was an old dog,
Too grey and tired for tears,
He lay outside the house-door
And watched for twenty years.

When twenty years were ended
Ulysses came from Troy.
Argus wagged an old dog's wag,
And then he died for joy.

Eleanor Farjeon

245

Soarfish the Swordfish

The swordfish saws
through the grain
of each wave

Storing the off-cuts
in his
decorative cave

There he sands
wooden knick-knacks
he's carved for himself

Which he proudly
displays on a
waterproof shelf

He chisels
and whittles and
varnishes things

Like wardrobes
and mountains and
oak angel wings

If you walk
on a beach
with no driftwood around

And you're slightly
aware of a
faint, grating sound

Put your ear
to the ocean
and you'll hear I suppose

The tone of
the swordfish
sharpening his nose.

Stewart Henderson

The Dark Wood

In the dark, dark wood, there was
   a dark, dark house,
And in that dark, dark house, there was
   a dark, dark room,
And in the dark, dark room, there was
   a dark, dark cupboard,
And in that dark, dark cupboard there was
   a dark, dark shelf,
And on that dark, dark shelf there was
   a dark, dark box,
And in that dark, dark box, there was a
   GHOST!

Anon.

The Way through the Woods

They shut the road through the woods
Seventy years ago.
Weather and rain have undone it again,
And now you would never know
There was once a road through the woods
Before they planted the trees.
It is underneath the coppice and heath,
And the thin anemones.
Only the keeper sees
That, where the ring-dove broods,
And the badgers roll at ease,
There was once a road through the woods.

Yet, if you enter the woods
Of a summer evening late,
When the night-air cools on the trout-ringed pools
Where the otter whistles his mate,
(They fear not men in the woods,
Because they see so few.)
You will hear the beat of a horse's feet,
And the swish of a skirt in the dew,
Steadily cantering through
The misty solitudes,
As though they perfectly knew
The old lost road through the woods . . .
But there is no road through the woods.

Rudyard Kipling

Aliens Stole My Underpants

To understand the ways
of alien beings is hard,
and I've never worked it out
why they landed in my backyard.

And I've always wondered why
on their journey from the stars,
these aliens stole my underpants
and took them back to Mars.

They came on Monday night
when the weekend wash had been done,
pegged out on the line
to be dried by the morning sun.

Mrs Driver from next door
was a witness at the scene
when aliens snatched my underpants –
I'm glad that they were clean!

It seems they were quite choosy
as nothing else was taken.
Do aliens wear underpants
or were they just mistaken?

I think I have a theory
as to what they wanted them for,
they needed to block off a draught
blowing in through the spacecraft door.

Or maybe some Mars museum
wanted items brought back from space.
Just think, my pair of Y-fronts
displayed in their own glass case.

And on the label beneath
would be written where they got 'em
and how such funny underwear
once covered an Earthling's bottom!

Brian Moses

Cargoes

Quinquireme of Nineveh from distant Ophir
Rowing home to haven in sunny Palestine
With a cargo of ivory,
And apes and peacocks,
Sandalwood, cedarwood, and sweet white wine.

Stately Spanish galleon coming from the Isthmus,
Dipping through the Tropics by the palm-green shores,
With a cargo of diamonds,
Emeralds, amethysts,
Topazes, and cinnamon, and gold moidores.

Dirty British coaster with a salt-caked smoke stack
Butting through the Channel in the mad March days,
With a cargo of Tyne coal,
Road-rail, pig-lead,
Firewood, iron-ware, and cheap tin trays.

John Masefield

Dragon

Look very lightly
look that way –
I saw a dragon there
yesterday;

His ears were open,
his eyes were shut,
his scales were as hard
as a coconut.

His body was thick,
his tail was strong,
it stretched round the railings
ten feet long . . .

His snores were thunderous,
dark and deep.
He breathed like an engine
in his sleep.

Look through your lashes
faint and small . . .
Can you see anyone
there at all,

Down by the railings,
way-away?
I saw a dragon there
yesterday.

Jean Kenward

23

The Shark

A treacherous monster is the Shark
He never makes the least remark.

And when he sees you on the sand,
He doesn't seem to want to land.

He watches you take off your clothes,
And not the least excitement shows.

His eyes do not grow bright or roll,
He has astounding self-control.

He waits till you are quite undrest,
And seems to take no interest.

And when towards the sea you leap,
He looks as if he were asleep.

But when you once get in his range,
His whole demeanour seems to change.

He throws his body right about,
And his true character comes out.

It's no use crying or appealing,
He seems to lose all decent feeling.

After this warning you will wish
To keep clear of this treacherous fish.

His back is black, his stomach white,
He has a very dangerous bite.

Lord Alfred Douglas

Come on into my Tropical Garden

Come on into my tropical garden
Come on in and have a laugh in
Taste my sugar cake and my pine drink
Come on in please come on in

And yes you can stand up in my hammock
and breeze out in my trees
you can pick my hibiscus
and kiss my chimpanzees

O you can roll up in the grass
and if you pick up a flea
I'll take you down for a quick dip-wash
in the sea
believe me there's nothing better
for getting rid of a flea
than having a quick dip-wash in the sea

Come on into my tropical garden
Come on in please come on in

Grace Nichols

Macavity: The Mystery Cat

Macavity's a Mystery Cat: he's called the Hidden Paw –
For he's the master criminal who can defy the Law.
He's the bafflement of Scotland Yard, the Flying Squad's
despair:
For when they reach the scene of crime – *Macavity's not
there*!

Macavity, Macavity, there's no one like Macavity,
He's broken every human law, he breaks the law of gravity.
His powers of levitation would make a fakir stare,
And when you reach the scene of crime – *Macavity's not
      there*!
You may seek him in the basement, you may look up in the
      air –
But I tell you once and once again, *Macavity's not there*!

Macavity's a ginger cat, he's very tall and thin;
You would know him if you saw him, for his eyes are
      sunken in.
His brow is deeply lined with thought, his head is highly
      domed;
His coat is dusty from neglect, his whiskers are uncombed.
He sways his head from side to side, with movements like a
      snake;
And when you think he's half asleep, he's always wide
      awake.

Macavity, Macavity, there's no one like Macavity,
For he's a fiend in feline shape, a monster of depravity.
You may meet him in a by-street, you may see him in the
      square –
But when a crime's discovered, then *Macavity's not there*!

He's outwardly respectable. (They say he cheats at cards.)
And his footprints are not found in any file of Scotland
   Yard's.
And when the larder's looted, or the jewel-case is rifled,
Or when the milk is missing, or another Peke's been stifled,
Or the greenhouse glass is broken, and the trellis past
   repair –
Ay, there's the wonder of the thing! *Macavity's not there!*

And when the Foreign Office find a Treaty's gone astray,
Or the Admiralty lose some plans and drawings by the way,
There may be a scrap of paper in the hall or on the stair –
But it's useless to investigate – *Macavity's not there!*
And when the loss has been disclosed, the Secret Service say:
'It *must* have been Macavity!' – but he's a mile away.
You'll be sure to find him resting, or a-licking of his thumbs,
Or engaged in doing complicated long division sums.

Macavity, Macavity, there's no one like Macavity,
There never was a Cat of such deceitfulness and suavity.
He always has an alibi, and one or two to spare:
At whatever time the deed took place – MACAVITY WASN'T
   THERE!
And they say that all the Cats whose wicked deeds are
   widely known
(I might mention Mungojerrie, I might mention
   Griddlebone)
Are nothing more than agents for the Cat who all the time
Just controls their operations: the Napoleon of Crime!

T.S. Eliot

The Gardener

The gardener stood at the garden gate,
  A primrose in his hand;
He saw a lovely girl come by,
  Slim as a willow wand

'O lady, can you fancy me,
  And will you share my life?
All my garden flowers are yours,
  If you will be my wife.

'The white lily will be your shirt
  It suits your body best;
With cornflowers in your hair,
  A red rose on your breast.

'Your gloves will be the marigold,
  Glittering on your hand;
Your dress will be the sweet-william
  That grows upon the bank.'

'Young man, I cannot be your wife;
  I fear it will not do.
Although you care for me,' she said,
  'I cannot care for you.

'As you've provided clothes for me
  Among the summer flowers,
So I'll provide some clothes for you
  Among the winter showers.

'The fallen snow will be your shirt,
  It suits your body best;
Your head will be wound with the eastern wind,
  With the cold rain on your breast.

'Your boots will be of the seaweed
  That drifts upon the tide;
Your horse will be the white wave –
  Leap on, young man, and ride!'

Anon.

Solomon Grundy

Solomon Grundy,
Born on a Monday,
Christened on Tuesday,
Married on Wednesday,
Took ill on Thursday,
Worse on Friday,
Died on Saturday,
Buried on Sunday.
That was the end
Of Solomon Grundy.

Anon.

Remember

Remember me when I am gone away,
   Gone far away into the silent land;
   When you can no more hold me by the hand
Nor I half turn to go yet turning stay.
Remember me when no more day by day
   You tell me of our future that you planned:
   Only remember me; you understand
It will be late to counsel then or pray.
Yet if you should forget me for a while
   And afterwards remember, do not grieve:
   For if the darkness and corruption leave
   A vestige of the thoughts that once I had,
Better by far you should forget and smile
   Than that you should remember and be sad.

Christina Rossetti

29

The Mysteries of Nature
(or Globular Bunkular My Duck Has Sunkular)

Nature poems are popular
but seldom very jocular
But this one is spectacular
because it's quite funicular

Let's take a country walkular
through fields that are rusticular
look through your binocular
there's an eagle and a hawkular

The hedgerow in particular
is a home so very insular
for creatures shaped triangular
or even semi-circular

You may come across a spookular
in the forest deep and darkular
a sharp stab in your jugular
means you've met up with Count Dracular

By the church that looks so secular
there is a pond where you'll find duckular
this one doesn't quackular
since it argued with a truckular

I see by the town clockular
that time is passing quickular
I think I need a breakular
too much nature makes you sickular

John Rice

Mr and Mrs Lilac

Never go to the Lilacs' house
to fetch back your ball.
The Lilacs don't like children.
They don't like children at all.

Mr and Mrs Lilac steal children's balls.
They've got my balls, they got my pals'.
Mr Lilac loathes you ringing his bell.
He says, 'It's my ball now, my ball.'

Mr Lilac smiles a terrible smile.
He watches you shake and tremble.
Mrs Lilac says, 'It's our land, dear.
Our land. You should be careful.'

Once I peeped through their window.
The moon shone on my shadow.
Inside the Lilacs were playing ball.
There was haunting music in the hall.

An orange light glowed in the room.
Their faces were bright as broom.
Mr Lilac passed Mrs Lilac my basketball.
Mrs Lilac passed Mr Lilac Mugsy's rugby ball.

The strange thing was all our balls
looked new again, through the window.
Lisa's leather football, still bright white.
Django's tennis ball, bright yellow tonight.

Nasreen's new golf balls, Jodie's bouncy balls,
Billy's baseballs, Pili's ping-pong balls.
I heard Mrs Lilac laugh through the window.
'Good throw, Mr Lilac, good throw.'

Jackie Kay

Careless Rambles

I love to wander at my idle will
In summer's luscious prime about the fields
And kneel when thirsty at the little rill
To sip the draught its pebbly bottom yields
And where the maple bush its fountain shields
To lie and rest a swailey hour away
And crop the swelling peascod from the land
Or mid the uplands woodland walks to stray
Where oaks for aye o'er their old shadows stand
Neath whose dark foliage with a welcome hand
I pluck the luscious strawberry ripe and red
As beauty's lips – and in my fancy's dreams
As mid the velvet moss I musing tread
Feel life as lovely as her picture seems.

John Clare

August

Ozymandias

I met a traveller from an antique land
Who said: Two vast and trunkless legs of stone
Stand in the desert. Near them, on the sand,
Half sunk, a shattered visage lies, whose frown,
And wrinkled lip, and sneer of cold command
Tell that its sculptor well those passions read
Which yet survive (stamped on these lifeless things)
The hand that mocked them and the heart that fed:
And on the pedestal these words appear:
'My name is Ozymandias, King of Kings:
Look on my works, ye Mighty, and despair!'
Nothing beside remains. Round the decay
Of that colossal wreck, boundless and bare
The lone and level sands stretch far away.

Percy Bysshe Shelley

The Song of the Mischievous Dog

There are many who say that a dog has its day,
   And a cat has a number of lives;
There are others who think that a lobster is pink,
   And that bees never work in their hives.
There are fewer, of course, who insist that a horse
   Has a horn and two humps on its head,
And a fellow who jests that a mare can build nests
   Is as rare as a donkey that's red.
Yet in spite of all this, I have moments of bliss,
   For I cherish a passion for bones,
And though doubtful of biscuit, I'm willing to risk it,
   And I love to chase rabbits and stones.
But my greatest delight is to take a good bite
   At a calf that is plump and delicious;
And if I indulge in a bite at a bulge,
   Let's hope you won't think me too vicious.

Dylan Thomas

from *Jubilate Agno*

For I will consider my Cat Jeoffrey.

For he is the servant of the Living God, duly and daily serving him.

For at the first glance of the glory of God in the East, he worships in his way.

For this is done by wreathing his body seven times round with elegant quickness.

For then he leaps up to catch the musk, which is the blessing of God upon his prayer.

For he rolls upon the prank to work it in.

For having done duty and received blessing he begins to consider himself.

For this he performs in ten degrees.

For first he looks upon his forepaws, to see if they are clean.

For secondly he kicks up behind to clear away there.

For thirdly he works it upon stretch with the forepaws extended.

For fourthly he sharpens his paws by wood.

For fifthly he washes himself.

For sixthly he rolls upon wash.

For seventhly he fleas himself, that he may not be interrupted upon the beat.

For eighthly he rubs himself against a post.

For ninthly he looks up for his instructions.

For tenthly he goes in quest of food.

For having considered God and himself he will consider his neighbour.

For if he meets another cat he will kiss her in kindness.

For when he takes his prey he plays with it to give it chance.

For one mouse in seven escapes by his dallying.

For when his day's work is done his business more properly begins.

For he keeps the Lord's watch in the night against the adversary.

For he counteracts the powers of darkness by his electrical skin and glaring eyes.

For he counteracts the Devil, who is death, by brisking about the life.

For in his morning orisons he loves the sun and the sun loves him.

For he is of the tribe of Tiger.

For the Cherub Cat is a term of the Angel Tiger.

Christopher Smart

The Octopus

Tell me, O Octopus, I begs,
Is those things arms, or is they legs?
I marvel at thee, Octopus;
If I were thou, I'd call me Us.

Ogden Nash

Fruits

Half a pawpaw in the basket –
Only one o' we can have it.
Wonder which one that will be?
I have a feeling that is me.

One guinep in the tree
Hanging down there tempting me.
It don' mek no sense to pick it,
One guinep can't feed a cricket.

Two ripe guava pon the shelf,
I know I hid them there meself.
When night com an' it get dark
Me an' them will have a talk.

Three sweet-sop, well I jus' might
Give on o' them a nice big bite.
Cover up the bite jus' so, sis,
Then no one will ever notice.

Four red apple near me chair –
Who so careless put them there?
Them don' know how me love apple?
Well, thank God fer silly people.

Five jew-plum, I can't believe it!
How they know jew-plum's me fav'rit?
But why they hide them in a cupboard?
Cho, people can be so awkward.

August

Six naseberry, you want a nibble?
Why baby must always dribble?
Come wipe you mout', it don't mek sense
To broadcast the evidence.

Seven mango! What a find!
The smaddy who lef them really kind.
One fe you an' six fe me,
If you want more, climb the tree.

Eight orange fe cousin Clem,
But I have just one problem –
How to get rid o' the eight skin
That the orange them come in.

Nine jackfruit! Not even me
Can finish nine, but let me see,
I don't suppose that they will miss one.
That was hard, but now me done.

Ten banana, mek them stay,
I feeling really full today.
Mek me lie down on me bed, quick.
Lawd, ah feeling really sick.

Valerie Bloom

Sergeant Brown's Parrot

Many policemen wear upon their shoulders
Cunning little radios. To pass away the time
They talk about the traffic to them, listen to the news,
And it helps them to Keep Down Crime.

But Sergeant Brown, he wears upon his shoulder
A tall green parrot as he's walking up and down
And all the parrot says is 'Who's-a-pretty-boy-then?'
'I am,' says Sergeant Brown.

Kit Wright

Burglars

'I heard something downstairs,' she said.
'What was it?' I said.
'I don't know,' she said.
'Maybe it's a noise,' I said.
'Go down and see,' she said.
'You mean, go down and see?' I said.
'Yes,' she said.
'Right now?' I said.
'Yes,' she said.
'It was probably a twig scraping the window,' I said.
'There are no trees outside our house,' she said.
'I think it has stopped,' I said.
'In that case, go down and see,' she said.
'If it is a burglar,' I said,
'I may disturb him,' I said.
'What do you mean *him*?' she said.
'Women can be burglars too,' she said.

Steve Turner

Give Me a House

Give me a house, said Polly.
Give me land, said Hugh.
Give me the moon, said Sadie.
Give me the sun, said Sue.

Give me a horse, said Rollo.
Give me a hound, said Joe.
Give me fine linen, said Sarah.
Give me silk, said Flo.

Give me a mountain, said Kirsty.
Give me a valley, said Jim.
Give me a river, said Dodo.
Give me the sky, said Tim.

Give me the ocean, said Adam.
Give me a ship, said Hal.
Give me a kingdom, said Rory.
Give me a crown, said Sal.

Give me gold, said Peter.
Give me silver, said Paul.
Give me love, said Jenny,
Or nothing at all.

Charles Causley

Rushing

Rush, rush, rush, rush,
Do we have to go so fast?
In a hurry, in a hurry,
Does it matter if we're last?
Quick, quick, quick, quick,
My forehead and my ankles ache.
Speedy, speedy, speedy, speedy,
Can't we stop and have a break?
Run, run, run, run,
We can catch another bus.
Puff, puff, puff, puff,
No breath left at all in us.
Slow, slow, slow, slow,
Things to look at while we wait.
Chat, chat, chat, chat,
It's much nicer being late.

Michelle Magorian

When that I was
and a little tiny boy

When that I was and a little tiny boy,
   With hey, ho, the wind and the rain;
A foolish thing was but a toy,
   For the rain it raineth every day.

But when I came to man's estate,
   With hey, ho, the wind and the rain;
'Gainst knaves and thieves men shut their gates,
   For the rain it raineth every day.

But when I came, alas! to wive,
   With hey, ho, the wind and the rain;
By swaggering could I never thrive,
   For the rain it raineth every day.

But when I came unto my beds,
   With hey, ho, the wind and the rain;
With toss-pots still had drunken heads,
   For the rain it raineth every day.

A great while ago the world begun,
  With hey, ho, the wind and the rain;
But that's all one, our play is done,
  And we strive to please you every day.

William Shakespeare

Dazzledance
(for Heather)

I have an eye of silver,
I have an eye of gold,
I have a tongue of reed-grass
  and a story to be told.

I have a hand of metal,
I have a hand of clay,
I have two arms of granite,
  and a song for every day.

I have a foot of damson,
I have a foot of corn,
I have two legs of leaf-stalk
   and a dance as yet unborn.

I have a dream of water,
I have a dream of snow,
I have a thought of wildfire
   and a harp-string long and low.

I have an eye of silver,
I have an eye of gold,
I have a tongue of reed-grass
   and a story to be told.

John Rice

In Flanders Fields

In Flanders fields the poppies blow
Between the crosses, row on row,
    That mark our place; and in the sky
    The larks, still bravely singing, fly
Scarce heard amid the guns below.

We are the Dead. Short days ago
We lived, felt dawn, saw sunset glow,
    Loved and were loved, and now we lie
    In Flanders fields.

Take up our quarrel with the foe:
To you from failing hands we throw
    The torch; be yours to hold it high.
    If ye break faith with us who die
We shall not sleep, though poppies grow
    In Flanders fields.

John McCrae

Minnie and Winnie

Minnie and Winnie
  Slept in a shell.
Sleep, little ladies!
  And they slept well.

Pink was the shell within,
  Silver without;
Sounds of the great sea
  Wandered about.

Sleep, little ladies,
  Wake not soon!
Echo on echo
  Dies to the moon.

Two bright stars
  Peeped into the shell.
'What are they dreaming of?
  Who can tell?'

Started a green linnet
Out of the croft;
Wake, little ladies,
The sun is aloft!

Alfred Lord Tennyson

Silver

Slowly, silently, now the moon
Walks the night in her silver shoon;
This way, and that, she peers, and sees
Silver fruit upon silver trees;
One by one the casements catch
Her beams beneath the silvery thatch;
Couched in his kennel, like a log,
With paws of silver sleeps the dog;
From their shadowy cote the white breasts peep
Of doves in a silver-feathered sleep;
A harvest mouse goes scampering by,
With silver claws, and a silver eye;
And moveless fish in the water gleam
By silver reeds in a silver stream.

Walter de la Mare

Awake in the Siesta

Rumours of winds and dusty afternoons,
Others' siesta, I stay wideawake,
The only conscious one here. All cats sleep
Upon their shadows. Hot against the walls
Leaves and butterflies lick the crumbling stone.
Here was I, all by myself and happy,
Content in a country truly my first home.
So Tuscany about six years ago,
In a small town never sought out by tourists,
Nothing important, no mosaics and only
One small church not worth the sight-seer's inspection.
The view from my window was peerless, the shutters wide.
Everything I could possess but no possession.
I laid myself open to the atmosphere,
Dipped my hands in water.
                              Tuscany
You are a sweetness in nostrils still,
A view I'd never trade, and, every morning
The promising haze and the emerging hills.

Elizabeth Jennings

If You Should Meet a Crocodile

If you should meet a crocodile,
   Don't take a stick and poke him;
Ignore the welcome in his smile,
   Be careful not to stroke him.
For he sleeps upon the Nile,
   He thinner gets and thinner;
But whene'er you meet a crocodile
   He's ready for his dinner.

Anon.

Girl From a Train

We stopped by a cornfield
Near Shrewsbury
A girl in a sun hat
Smiled at me.

Then I was seven
Now sixty-two
Wherever you are
I remember you.

Gareth Owen

The Donkey

I saw a donkey
One day old,
His head was too big
For his neck to hold;
His legs were shaky
And long and loose,
They rocked and staggered
And weren't much use.

He tried to gambol
And frisk a bit,
But he wasn't quite sure
Of the trick of it.
His queer little coat
Was soft and grey,
And curled at his neck
In a lovely way.

His face was wistful
And left no doubt
That he felt life needed
Some thinking about.
So he blundered round
In venturesome quest,
And then lay flat
On the ground to rest.

He looked so little
And weak and slim,
I prayed the world
Might be good to him.

Anon.

It's Dark in Here

I am writing these poems
From inside a lion,
And it's rather dark in here.
So please excuse the handwriting
Which may not be too clear.
But this afternoon by the lion's cage
I'm afraid I got too near.
And I'm writing these lines
From inside a lion,
And it's rather dark in here.

Shel Silverstein

Where go the Boats?

Dark brown is the river,
  Golden is the sand.
It flows along for ever,
  With trees on either hand.

Green leaves a-floating,
  Castles of the foam,
Boats of mine a-boating –
  Where will all come home?

On goes the river,
  And out past the mill,
Away down the valley,
  Away down the hill.

Away down the river,
  A hundred miles or more,
Other little children
  Shall bring my boats ashore.

Robert Louis Stevenson

The White Cat of Trenarren
(for Beryl Cloke)

He was a mighty hunter in his youth
At Polmear all day on the mound, on the pounce
For anything moving, rabbit or bird or mouse –
  My cat and I grow old together.

After a day's hunting he'd come into the house
Delicate ears stuck all with fleas.
At Trenarren I've heard his sigh with pleasure
After a summer's day in the long-grown leas –
  My cat and I grow old together.

When I was a child I played all day,
With only a little cat for companion,
At solitary games of my own invention
Under the table or up in the green bay –
  My cat and I grow old together.

When I was a boy I wandered the roads
Up to the downs by gaunt Carn Grey,
Wrapt in a dream at end of day,
All round me the moor, below me the bay –
  My cat and I grow old together.

Now we are too often apart, yet
Turning out of Central Park into the Plaza,
Or walking Michigan Avenue against the lake-wind,
I see a little white shade in the shrubbery
Of far-off Trenarren, never far from my mind –
   My cat and I grow old together.

When I come home from too much travelling,
Cautiously he comes out of his lair to my call,
Receives me at first with a shy reproach
At long absence to him incomprehensible
   My cat and I grow old together.

Incapable of much or long resentment,
He scratches at my door to be let out
In early morning in the ash moonlight,
Or red dawn breaking through Mother Bond's spinney –
   My cat and I grow old together.

No more frisking as of old,
Or chasing his shadow over the lawn,
But a dignified old person, tickling
His nose against twig or flower in the border,
Until evening falls and bed-time's in order,
Unable to keep eyes open any longer
He waits for me to carry him upstairs
To nestle all night snug at foot of bed –
   My cat and I grow old together.

Careful of his licked and polished appearance,
Ears like shell-whorls pink and transparent,
White plume waving proudly over the paths,
Against a background of sea and blue hydrangeas –
My cat and I grow old together.

A.L. Rowse

Can We Have Our Ball Back, Please?

England gave football to the world
Who, now they've got the knack,
Play it better than we do
And won't let us have it back.

Gareth Owen

Wind Cat

Jeoffrey will not go out tonight,
Hovers by the cat-flap, paw uplifted,
Eyes wide and wild ears pricked
Listening to wind-cat prowling the earth.

Wind-cat assaults the cat-flap violently
With invisible paws,
But does not come in,
Does not have a smell,
But spits savagely in Jeoffrey's face,
Then retires to leap through the garden
Tearing and smashing fearsomely

At Jeoffrey's trees,
Making Jeoffrey's fence
Creak violently;
Transmitting his terrible size,
Then is back, rattling the flap,
Spitting again, a fearsome show.

Yet Jeoffrey
Is not entirely convinced,
How can so great a creature have no smell
But the usual grass, earth and trees?
Jeoffrey suspects a con
Until the cat next door,
The usual cat-flap burglar,
Terror of the road,
Streaks past the window
Cowering to the earth,
Soaked, blown and beaten
By the wind-cat's paws.

Jeoffrey seems to shrug,
Retires to the lounge
To wash, by the fire
And guard the house against
An infinitely smaller wind-cat
Burgling down the chimney.
He knows his limitations,
That's his strength.

Robert Westall

The Lurcher

Forth goes the woodman, leaving unconcerned
The cheerful haunts of men to wield the axe
And drive the wedge in yonder forest drear,
From morn to eve his solitary task.
Shaggy and lean and shrewd, with pointed ears
And tail cropped short, half-lurcher and half-cur,
His dog attends him. Close behind his heel
Now creeps he slow, and now with many a frisk
Wide scampering, snatches up the drifted snow
With ivory teeth, or ploughs it with his snout;
Then shakes his powder'd coat, and barks for joy.

William Cowper

Cats

Cats sleep
Anywhere,
Any table,
Any chair,

Top of piano
Window-ledge,
In the middle,
On the edge,
Open drawer,
Empty shoe,
Anybody's
Lap will do,
Fitted in a
Cardboard box,
In the cupboard
With your frocks –
Anywhere!
They don't care!
Cats sleep
Anywhere.

Eleanor Farjeon

Spells

I dance and dance without any feet –
This is the spell of the ripening wheat.

With never a tongue I've a tale to tell –
This is the meadow-grasses' spell.

I give you health without any fee –
This is the spell of the apple-tree.

I rhyme and riddle without any book –
This is the spell of the bubbling brook.

Without any legs I run for ever –
This is the spell of the mighty river.

I fall for ever and not at all –
This is the spell of the waterfall.

Without a voice I roar aloud –
This is the spell of the thunder-cloud.

No button or seam has my white coat –
This is the spell of the leaping goat.

I can cheat strangers with never a word –
This is the spell of the cuckoo-bird.

We have tongues in plenty but speak no names –
This is the spell of the fiery flames.

The creaking door has a spell to riddle –
I play a tune without any fiddle.

James Reeves

Way Down South

Way down South where bananas grow,
A grasshopper stepped on an elephant's toe.
The elephant said, with tears in his eyes,
'Pick on somebody your own size.'

Anon.

In the Orchard

There was a giant by the Orchard Wall,
Peeping about on this side and on that,
And feeling in the trees. He was as tall
As the big apple tree, and twice as fat:
His beard poked out, all bristly-black, and there
Were leaves and gorse and heather in his hair.

He held a blackthorn club in his right hand,
And plunged the other into every tree,
Searching for something – You could stand
Beside him and not reach up to his knee,
So big he was – I trembled lest he should
Come trampling, round-eyed, down to where I stood.

I tried to get away. – But, as I slid
Under a bush, he saw me, and he bent
Down deep at me, and said, '*Where is she hid?*'
I pointed over there, and off he went –

But, while he searched, I turned and simply flew
Round to the lilac bushes back to you.

James Stephens

Littlemouse

Light of day going,
Harvest moon glowing,
People beginning to snore,
Tawny owl calling,
Dead of night falling,
Littlemouse opening her door.

Scrabbling and tripping,
Sliding and slipping,
Over the ruts of the plough,
Under the field gate,
Mustn't arrive late,
Littlemouse hurrying now.

Into a clearing,
All the birds cheering,
Woodpecker blowing a horn,
Nightingale fluting,
Blackbird toot-tooting,
Littlemouse dancing till dawn.

Soon comes the morning,
No time for yawning,
Home again Littlemouse creeps,
Over the furrow,
Back to her burrow,
Into bed. Littlemouse sleeps.

Richard Edwards

August Ends

A nip in the air today, and autumn
Playing hide and seek with summer;
Winter takes a first grip on plant, insect, bird.
Last blackberry flowers fade,
And fruit, moving from green to red,
Dangles foot long purple clusters
Over downy hedgerows, wasps go numb,
Fall drowsy on dropped plums, honey and smoky wax
Perfume the spidered loft, barley shines.
Swifts on curved wings wheel overhead
Printing broad arrows on the leaden sky;
And now I catch the echo of the far north wind
And over the shorn and stubbled land
The dreaded hawk hovers, and a cloud of peewits cry.

Leonard Clark

Blackberry-Picking
For Philip Hobsbaum

Late August, given heavy rain and sun
For a full week, the blackberries would ripen.
At first, just one, a glossy purple clot
Among others, red, green, hard as a knot.
You ate that first one and its flesh was sweet
Like thickened wine: summer's blood was in it
Leaving stains upon the tongue and lust for
Picking. Then red ones inked up and that hunger
Sent us out with milk-cans, pea-tins, jam-pots
Where briars scratched and wet grass bleached our boots.
Round hayfields, cornfields and potato-drills
We trekked and picked until the cans were full,
Until the tinkling bottom had been covered
With green ones, and on top big dark blobs burned
Like a plate of eyes. Our hands were peppered
With thorn pricks, our palms sticky as Bluebeard's.

We hoarded the fresh berries in the byre.
But when the bath was filled we found a fur,
A rat-grey fungus, glutting on our cache.
The juice was stinking too. Once off the bush
The fruit fermented, the sweet flesh would turn sour.
I always felt like crying. It wasn't fair
That all the lovely canfuls smelt of rot.
Each year I hoped they'd keep, knew they would not.

Seamus Heaney

September

Autumn

Yellow the bracken,
   Golden the sheaves,
Rosy the apples,
   Crimson the leaves;
Mist on the hillside,
   Clouds grey and white.
Autumn, good morning!
   Summer, good night!

Florence Hoatson

The Meadow Mouse

I

In a shoe box stuffed in an old nylon stocking
Sleeps the baby mouse I found in the meadow,
Where he trembled and shook beneath a stick
Till I caught him up by the tail and brought him in,
Cradled in my hand,
A little quaker, the whole body of him trembling,
His absurd whiskers sticking out like a cartoon-mouse,
His feet like small leaves,
Little lizard-feet,
Whitish and spread wide when he tried to struggle away,
Wriggling like a miniscule puppy.

Now he's eaten his three kinds of cheese and drunk from his
    bottle-cap watering-trough –
So much he just lies in one corner,
His tail curled under him, his belly big
As his head, his bat-like ears
Twitching, tilting toward the least sound.

Do I imagine he no longer trembles
When I come close to him?
He seems no longer to tremble.

II

But this morning the shoe-box house on the back porch is
    empty.
Where has he gone, my meadow mouse,
My thumb of a child that nuzzled in my palm? –
To run under the hawk's wing,
Under the eye of the great owl watching from the elm-tree,
To live by courtesy of the shrike, the snake, the tom-cat.

I think of the nestling fallen into the deep grass,
The turtle gasping in the dusty rubble of the highway,
The paralytic stunned in the tub, and the water rising, –
All things innocent, hapless, forsaken.

                                          Theodore Roethke

Autumn

Season of conkers and fireworks
and mellow fruitfulness. New shoes,
and a coat that's a bit too big,
to grow into next year. Blackberries
along the canal, white jungles
of frost on the window. Leaves
to kick all the way home,
the smell of bonfires,
stamping the ice on puddles
into crazy paving. The nights come in
early, and you can't play out
after school. Soon
there'll be tangerines in the shops,
in shiny paper like Christmas lights.

The little ones write letters to Santa Claus.

The big ones laugh under the streetlights.

Adrian Henri

To Autumn

Season of mists and mellow fruitfulness,
  Close bosom-friend of the maturing sun,
Conspiring with him how to load and bless
  With fruit the vines that round the thatch-eaves run;
To bend with apples the mossed cottage-trees,
  And fill all fruit with ripeness to the core;
    To swell the gourd, and plump the hazel shells
With a sweet kernel; to set budding more,
  And still more, later flowers for the bees,
  Until they think warm days will never cease,
    For summer has o'er-brimmed their clammy cells.

Who hath not seen thee oft amid thy store?
  Sometimes whoever seeks abroad may find
Thee sitting careless on a granary floor,
  Thy hair soft-lifted by the winnowing wind;
Or on a half-reaped furrow sound asleep,
  Drowsed with the fume of poppies, while thy hook
    Spares the next swath and all its twinèd flowers;
And sometimes like a gleaner thou dost keep
  Steady thy laden head across a brook;
Or by a cider-press, with patient look,
    Thou watchest the last oozings hours by hours.

September

Where are the songs of spring? Aye, where are they?
  Think not of them, thou hast thy music too –
While barred clouds bloom the soft-dying day,
  And touch the stubble-plains with rosy hue;
Then in a wailful choir the small gnats mourn
  Among the river sallows, borne aloft
    Or sinking as the light wind lives or dies;
And full-grown lambs loud bleat from hilly bourn;
  Hedge-crickets sing; and now with treble soft
The redbreast whistles from a garden-croft;
  And gathering swallows twitter in the skies.

John Keats

Superman's Dog

Superman's dog – he's the best
Helping pets in distress
Red and gold pants and vest
'SD' on his chest

Superman's dog – X-ray sight
Green bones filled with Kryptonite
Bright blue lycra tights in flight
Faster than a meteorite

Better than Batman's robin
Rougher than Robin's bat
Faster than Spiderman's spider
Cooler than Catwoman's cat

Superman's dog – bionic scent
Crime prevention – his intent
Woof and tough – cement he'll dent
What's his name – Bark Kent!

Paul Cookson

First Day at School

A millionbillionwillion miles from home
Waiting for the bell to go. (To go where?)
Why are they all so big, other children?
So noisy? So much at home they
must have been born in uniform.
Lived all their lives in playgrounds.
Spent the years inventing games
that don't let me in. Games
that are rough, that swallow you up.

And the railings.
All around, the railings.
Are they to keep out wolves and monsters?
Things that carry off and eat children?
Things you don't take sweets from?
Perhaps they're to stop us getting out.
Running away from the lessins. Lessin.
What does a lessin look like?
Sounds small and slimy.
They keep them in glassrooms.
Whole rooms made out of glass. Imagine.

I wish I could remember my name.
Mummy said it would come in useful.
Like wellies. When there's puddles.
Yellowwellies. I wish she was here.
I think my name is sewn on somewhere.
Perhaps the teacher will read it for me.
Tea-cher. The one who makes the tea.

Roger McGough

The Boy Who Dropped Litter

'ANTHONY WRIGGLY
SHAME ON YOU!'
screeched the teacher
as she spotted him
scrunching up his crisp packet
and dropping it carefully
on to the pavement outside school.

'If everyone went around
dropping crisp packets like you do
where would we be?'

(Anthony didn't know, so she told him)

'We'd be wading waist-high in crisp packets,
that's where!'

Anthony was silent.
He hung his head.

It looked to the teacher
as if he was very sorry.

When in fact he was trying to calculate
just how many packets it would take
to bring Basildon to a complete standstill.

Lindsay MacRae

New Shoes

I keep close to walls –
I go the back way –
They made me wear my
Stiff heavy best new
Shoes to school today.

They can't understand it,
I shouldn't be so silly –
But my old ones have got holes in
Or I'd never put these on:
They're just not *me*.

In my desk I sit with them
Tucked under my seat,
These big, bright, boat-size
Brand-new brogues I don't
Want anyone to meet.

– Such as our Miss Wilkins
Who'd look twice and say
As she goes past: 'My, my –
*Some*one's got some nice
New yellow shoes on today.'

September

I'm hiding in the cloakrooms
(No one's noticed yet),
With my feet under the benches . . .
I *won't* go out,
I'm trying to forget . . .

Like marble pedestals
They fix me to the spot.
Everywhere, I'm caught
In the act of wearing them,
Guilty, though I'm not.

Now I'm standing in the long grass
All on my own.
– I'd sooner have
The Emperor's
New clothes on.

Brian Lee

My Dog, Spot

I have a white dog
  Whose name is Spot,
And he's sometimes white
  And he's sometimes not.
But whether he's white
  Or whether he's not,
There's a patch on his ear
  That makes him Spot.

He has a tongue
  That is long and pink,
And he lolls it out
  When he wants to think,
He seems to think most
  When the weather is hot.
He's a wise sort of dog,
  Is my dog, Spot.

He likes a bone
  And he likes a ball,
But he doesn't care
  For a cat at all.
He waggles his tail
  And he knows what's what,
So I'm glad that he's my dog,
  My dog, Spot.

Rodney Bennett

The Plaint of the Camel

Canary-birds feed on sugar and seed,
  Parrots have crackers to crunch;
And as for the poodles, they tell me the noodles
  Have chicken and cream for their lunch.
But there's never a question
About MY digestion,
  ANYTHING does for me.

Cats, you're aware, can repose in a chair,
   Chickens can roost upon rails;
Puppies are able to sleep in a stable,
   And oysters can slumber in pails.
But no one supposes
A poor Camel dozes.
   ANY PLACE does for me.

Lambs are enclosed where it's never exposed,
   Coops are constructed for hens;
Kittens are treated to houses well heated.
   And pigs are protected by pens.
But a Camel comes handy
Wherever it's sandy,
   ANYWHERE does for me.

People would laugh if you rode a giraffe,
   Or mounted the back of an ox;
It's nobody's habit to ride on a rabbit,
   Or try to bestraddle a fox.
But as for a Camel, he's
Ridden by families –
   ANY LOAD does for me.

A snake is as round as a hole in the ground;
  Weasels are wavy and sleek;
And no alligator could ever be straighter
  Than lizards that live in a creek.
But a camel's all lumpy,
And bumpy, and humpy,
  ANY SHAPE does for me.

Charles Edward Carryl

He Wishes for the Cloths of Heaven

Had I the heavens' embroider'd cloths,
Enwrought with golden and silver light,
The blue and the dim and the dark cloths
Of night and light and the half light;
I would spread the cloths under your feet:
But I, being poor, have only my dreams;
I have spread my dreams under your feet;
Tread softly because you tread on my dreams.

W.B. Yeats

Give Yourself a Hug

Give yourself a hug
when you feel unloved

Give yourself a hug
when people put on airs
to make you feel a bug

Give yourself a hug
when everyone seems to give you
a cold-shoulder shrug

Give yourself a hug –
a big big hug

And keep on singing,
'Only one in a million like me
Only one in a million-billion-trillion-zillion
like me.'

Grace Nichols

It Was Long Ago

I'll tell you, shall I, something I remember?
Something that still means a great deal to me.
It was long ago.

A dusty road in summer I remember,
A mountain and an old house, and a tree
That stood, you know,

Behind the house. An old woman I remember
In a red shawl with a grey cat on her knee
Humming under a tree.

She seemed the oldest thing I can remember,
But then perhaps I was not more than three.
It was long ago.

I dragged on the dusty road, and I remember
How the old woman looked over the fence at me
And seemed to know

How it felt to be three, and called out, I remember,
'Do you like bilberries and cream for tea?'
I went under the tree

And while she hummed, and the cat purred, I remember
How she filled a saucer with berries and cream for me
So long ago,

Such berries and such cream as I remember
I never had seen before, and never see
Today, you know.

And that is almost all I can remember,
The house, the mountain, the grey cat on her knee,
Her red shawl, and the tree,

And the taste of the berries, the feel of the sun I remember,
And the smell of everything that used to be
So long ago,

Till the heat on the road outside again I remember,
And how the long dusty road seemed to have for me
No end, you know.

That is the farthest thing I can remember.
It won't mean much to you. It does to me.
Then I grew up, you see.

Eleanor Farjeon

This Little Poem

This little poem has five lines
and five words on every line.
I wrote it out five times
between five o'clock and five past nine
using five different pencils every time
and this little poem tells lies.

Ian McMillan

Sally

She was a dog-rose kind of girl:
elusive, scattery as petals;
scratchy sometimes, tripping you like briars.
She teased the boys
turning this way and that, not to be tamed
or taught any more than the wind.
Even in school the word 'ought'
had no meaning for Sally.
On dull days
she'd sit quiet as a mole at her desk
delving in thought.
But when the sun called
she was gone, running the blue day down
till the warm hedgerows prickled the dusk
and moths flickered out.

Her mother scolded; Dad
gave her the hazel-switch,
said her head was stuffed with feathers
and a starling tongue.
But they couldn't take the shine out of her.
Even when it rained
you felt the sun saved under her skin.
She'd a way of escape
laughing at you from the bright end of a tunnel,
leaving you in the dark.

Phoebe Hesketh

The Kitten at Play

See the kitten on the wall,
Sporting with the leaves that fall,
Withered leaves, one, two and three,
Falling from the elder-tree;
Through the calm and frosty air
Of the morning bright and fair.

See the kitten, how she starts,
Crouches, stretches, paws and darts;
With a tiger-leap half way
Now she meets her coming prey.
Lets it go as fast and then
Has it in her power again.

Now she works with three and four,
Like an Indian conjuror;
Quick as he in feats of art,
Gracefully she plays her part;
Yet were gazing thousands there,
What would little Tabby care?

William Wordsworth

From a Railway Carriage

Faster than fairies, faster than witches,
Bridges and houses, hedges and ditches;
And charging along like troops in a battle,
All through the meadows the horses and cattle:
All of the sights of the hill and the plain
Fly as thick as driving rain;
And ever again, in the wink of an eye,
Painted stations whistle by.

Here is a child who clambers and scrambles,
All by himself and gathering brambles;
Here is a tramp who stands and gazes;
And there is the green for stringing the daisies!
Here is a cart run away in the road
Lumping along with man and load;
And here is a mill, and there is a river:
Each a glimpse and gone for ever!

Robert Louis Stevenson

Quack, Quack!

We have two ducks. One blue. One black.
And when our blue duck goes 'Quack-quack'
our black duck quickly quack-quacks back.
The quacks Blue quacks make her quite a quacker
but Black is a quicker quacker-backer.

Dr Seuss

Autumn

Fragile, notice that
As autumn starts, a light
Frost crisps up at night
And next day, for a while,
White covers path and lawn.
'Autumn is here, it is,'
Sings the stoical blackbird
But by noon pure gold is tossed
On everything. Leaves fall
As if they meant to rise.
Nothing of nature's lost.
The birth, the blight of things,
The bud, the stretching wings.

Elizabeth Jennings

A Small Dragon

I've found a small dragon in the woodshed.
Think it must have come from deep inside a forest
because it's damp and green and leaves
are still reflecting in its eyes.

I fed it on many things, tried grass,
the roots of stars, hazel-nut and dandelion,
but it stared up at me as if to say, I need
foods you can't provide.

It made a nest among the coal,
not unlike a bird's but larger,
it is out of place here
and is quite silent.

If you believed in it I would come
hurrying to your house to let you share my wonder,
but I want instead to see
if you yourself will pass this way.

Brian Patten

A Parroty of a Poem

The carpet fights
and squawks all night.
It swears and
chews the door.
I wonder if Dad
spelt it right
when he ordered
parakeet floor?

David Clayton

Autumn Gale

A Dickens of a day! You can't tell leaves
from birds – panicky things
hurtling past windows. Everything's
having a rough time. Hedges shivering
with fright: that plastic bag
tugging to free itself from the barbs
of the blackthorn, this back-garden willow
taking such stick it's nearly thrashed
out of its wits. Some big bully
is terrorizing the neighbourhood,
huffing and puffing to blow your house down.

Matt Simpson

How doth the little crocodile

How doth the little crocodile
  Improve his shining tail,
And pour the waters of the Nile
  On every golden scale!

How cheerfully he seems to grin,
  How neatly spreads his claws,
And welcomes little fishes in
  With gently smiling jaws!

Lewis Carroll

Daughter of the Sea

bog seeper
moss creeper
growing restless   getting steeper

trickle husher
swish and rusher
stone leaper   splash and gusher

foam flicker
mirror slicker
pebble pusher   boulder kicker

still pool
don't be fooled
shadow tricker   keeping cool

leap lunger
crash plunger
free fall   with thunder under

garbage binner
dump it in her
never mind her   dog's dinner

plastic bagger
old lagger
oil skinner   wharf nagger

cargo porter
weary water
tide dragger   long lost daughter

of the sea
the sea the sea
has caught her   up in its arms and set her free

Philip Gross

It's Only the Storm

'What's that creature that rattles the roof?'
'Hush, it's only the storm.'

'What's blowing the tiles and the branches off?'
'Hush, it's only the storm.'

'What's riding the sky like a wild white horse,
Flashing its teeth and stamping its hooves?'

'Hush, my dear, it's only the storm,
Racing the darkness till it catches the dawn.
Hush, my dear, it's only the storm,
When you wake in the morning, it will be gone.'

David Greygoose

Soldier, Soldier, Will You Marry Me?

Oh, soldier, soldier, will you marry me,
With your musket, fife and drum?
 Oh no, pretty maid, I cannot marry you,
 For I have no coat to put on.

Then away she went to the tailor's shop
As fast as legs could run,
And bought him one of the very very best,
And the soldier put it on.

Oh, soldier, soldier, will you marry me,
With your musket, fife and drum?
 Oh no, pretty maid, I cannot marry you,
 For I have no shoes to put on.

Then away she went to the cobbler's shop
As fast as legs could run,
And bought him a pair of the very very best,
And the soldier put them on.

Oh, soldier, soldier, will you marry me,
With your musket, fife and drum?
   Oh no, pretty maid, I cannot marry you,
   For I have a wife at home.

Anon.

Octopus or Octopuss

He doesn't miaow
he doesn't purr
the Octopus
in his undersea lair.
He's not quite awake
and he doesn't quite sleep.
A drifting, fringed, lampshade
in the dusk
of the deep.
He's the shape
which gulps fear
into each snorkelling tourist.
And he's far
too much work
for a manicurist.
He never intends
to cause
such a fuss.
But never
play cards
with an octopus.

Stewart Henderson

Haircut Rap

Ah sey, ah want it short,
Short back an' side,
Ah tell him man, ah tell him
When ah teck him aside,
Ah sey, ah want a haircut
Ah can wear with pride,
So lef' it long on top
But short back an' side.

Ah sey try an' put a pattern
In the shorter part,
Yuh could put a skull an' crossbone,
Or an arrow, through a heart,
Meck sure ah have enough hair lef'
Fe cover me wart,
Lef' likkle pon the top,
But the res' – keep it short.

Well, bwoy, him start to cut,
An' me settle down to wait,
Him was cuttin' from seven
Till half-past eight,
Ah was startin' to get worried
'Cause ah see it gettin' late,
But then him put the scissors down
Sey, 'There yuh are, mate.'

Well ah did see a skull an a
Criss-cross bone or two,
But was me own skull an bone
That was peepin' through
Ah looks jus' like a monkey
Ah did see once at the zoo,
Him sey, 'What's de matter, Tammy,
Don't yuh like the hair-do?'

Well, ah feel me heart stop beatin'
When me look pon me reflection,
Ah feel like somet'ing frizzle up
Right in me middle section
Ah look aroun' fe somewhey
Ah could crawl into an' hide
The day ah mek me brother cut
Me hair short back an' side.

Valerie Bloom

Registration

Emma Hackett?
Here, Miss!
Billy McBone?
Here, Miss!
Derek Drew?
Here, Miss!
Margaret Thatcher?
Still here, Miss!

Long John Silver?
Buccaneer, Miss!
Al Capone?
Racketeer, Miss!
Isambard Kingdom Brunel?
Engineer, Miss!
Davy Crockett?
Wild frontier, Miss!
Frank Bruno?
Cauliflower ear, Miss!

The White Rabbit?
Late, Miss!
Billy the Kid?
Infants, Miss!
Simple Simon?
Here, Sir!
Father Christmas?
Present (for you), Miss!

Count Dracula?
1, 2, 3, 4, Miss!
Necks door, Miss!
Dentists!

The Invisible Man?
Nowhere, Miss!
Almighty God?
Everywhere, Miss!
Tarzan?
Aaaaaaaaaah! Miss.
Sleeping Beauty?
Zzz, Miss.

Allan Ahlberg

The Barkday Party

For my dog's birthday party
I dressed like a bear.
My friends came as lions
and tigers and wolves and monkeys.
At first, Runabout couldn't believe
the bear was really me. But
he became his old self again
when I fitted on his magician's top hat.
Runabout became the star, running about
jumping up on chairs and tables
barking at every question asked him.
Then, in their ordinary clothes,
my friend Brian and his dad arrived
with their boxer, Skip. And with us
knowing nothing about it, Brian's dad
mixed the dog's party meat and milk
with wine he brought. We started
singing. Runabout started to yelp.
All the other six dogs joined –
yelping:

September

Happy Barkday to you
Happy Barkday to you
Happy Barkday Runabout
Happy Barkday to you!

James Berry

October

Patchwork Rap

I'm a touch lazy
Don't like doing much work
But I often get the itch
To pitch into some patchwork
It may be a hotchpotch
Like fretwork or such work
When I slouch on my couch
And I fetch out my patchwork

First I snatch a patch
From the batch in my pouch
But the patch doesn't match
The patches on my patchwork
So I catch another patch
From the batch in my satchel
And this one matches
The patches on my patchwork.
So I take my patch
And attach it with stitches
Patch against patch
Where the patchwork matches
But if it doesn't match
Even after it's attached
Then the mismatched stitch
Has to be detached.

I don't like thatchwork
Don't like ditchwork
Only kind I favour
Is my patchwork stitchwork
And soon my patchwork's
Going like clockwork
Sharper than a pitchfork
Neater than brickwork
Hotter than a firework
Cooler than a waxwork.

So I snatch a patch
From the batch in my pouch
But the patch doesn't match
The patches on my patchwork
So I catch another patch
From the batch in my satchel
And this one matches
The patches on my patchwork.
So I take my patch
And attach it with stitches
Patch against patch
Where the patchwork matches
And I keep on patching
Till everything's matching
And I keep on stitching
Till I've filled up the kitchen
With my rich rich rich
Wider than a soccer pitch
Wonderful colourful patchwork quilt!
Now which stitch is which?

Adrian Mitchell

Wizard with the Ball

Young Arthur Merlin's spellbinding
His skills are crystal clear
A wizard with the ball
He makes it disappear!

Which is very useful in the opposition's penalty area.

Paul Cookson

The Three Foxes

Once upon a time there were three little foxes
Who didn't wear stockings, and they didn't wear sockses,
But they all had handkerchiefs to blow their noses,
And they kept their handkerchiefs in cardboard boxes.

They lived in the forest in three little houses,
And they didn't wear coats, and they didn't wear trousies.
They ran through the woods on their little bare tootsies,
And they played 'Touch last' with a family of mouses.

They didn't go shopping in the High Street shopses,
But caught what they wanted in the woods and copses.
They all went fishing, and they caught three wormses,
They went out hunting, and they caught three wopses.

They went to a Fair, and they all won prizes –
Three plum-puddingses and three mince-pieses.
They rode on elephants and swang on swingses,
And hit three coconuts at coconut shieses.

That's all that I know of the three little foxes
Who kept their handkerchiefs in cardboard boxes.
They lived in the forest in three little houses,
But they didn't wear coats and they didn't wear trousies,
And they didn't wear stockings and they didn't wear
    sockses.

A.A. Milne

My Mother Saw a Dancing Bear

My mother saw a dancing bear
By the schoolyard, a day in June.
The keeper stood with chain and bar
And whistle-pipe, and played a tune.

And bruin lifted up its head
And lifted up its dusty feet,
And all the children laughed to see
It caper in the summer heat.

They watched as for the Queen it died.
They watched it march. They watched it halt.
They heard the keeper as he cried,
'Now, roly-poly!' 'Somersault!'

And then, my mother said, there came
The keeper with a begging-cup,
The bear with burning coat of fur,
Shaming the laughter to a stop.

They paid a penny for the dance,
But what they saw was not the show;
Only, in bruin's aching eyes,
Far-distant forests, and the snow.

Charles Causley

The Painting Lesson

'What's THAT, dear?'
asked the new teacher.

'It's Mummy,' I replied.

'But mums aren't green and orange!
You really haven't TRIED.
You don't just paint in SPLODGES
– You're old enough to know
You need to THINK before you work . . .
Now – have another go.'

She helped me draw two arms and legs,
A face with sickly smile,
A rounded body, dark brown hair,
A hat – and, in a while,
She stood back (with her face bright pink):
'That's SO much better – don't you think?'

But she turned white
At ten to three
When an orange-green blob
Collected me.

'Hi, Mum!'

Trevor Harvey

A Tale of Two Citizens

I have a Russian friend who lives in Minsk
And wears a lofty hat of beaver skinsk,
(Which does not suit a man so tall and thinsk).
He has a frizzly beard upon his chinsk.
He keeps his britches up with safety pinsk.
  'They're so much better than those thingsk
  Called belts and brackeies, don't you thinksk?'
  You'll hear him say, the man from Minsk.

He has a Polish pal who's from Gdansk,
Who lives by selling drinksk to football fansk,
And cheese rolls, from a little caravansk.
(He finds it pleasanter than robbing banksk.)
He also uses pinsk to hold his pantsk.
  'Keep up one's pantsk with rubber bandsk!?
  It can't be donesk! It simply can'tsk!
  Not in Gdansk!' he'll say. 'No thanksk!'

They're so alikesk that strangers often thinksk
That they are brothers, yesk, or even twinsk.
'I live in Minsk but I was born in Omsk,'
Says one. His friend replies, 'That's where *I'm* fromsk!
Perhaps we're brothers after all, not friendsk.'
    So they wrote homesk and asked their mumsk
    But found they weren'tsk; so they shook handsk
    And left for Minsk, and for Gdansk.

Gerard Benson

7

Geraldine Giraffe

The
longest
ever
woolly
scarf
was
worn
by
Geraldine
Giraffe.
Around
her
neck
the
scarf
she
wound,
but
still
it
trailed
upon
the
ground.

Colin West

Magic Cat

My mum whilst walking through the door
Spilt some magic on the floor.
Blobs of this
and splots of that
but most of it upon the cat.

Our cat turned magic, straight away
and in the garden went to play
where it grew two massive wings
and flew around in fancy rings.
'Oh look!' cried Mother, pointing high,
'I didn't know our cat could fly.'
Then with a dash of Tibby's tail
she turned my mum into a snail!

So now she lives beneath a stone
and dusts around a different home.
And I'm an ant
and Dad's a mouse
And Tibby's living in our house.

Peter Dixon

If

If you can keep your head when all about you
Are losing theirs and blaming it on you,
If you can trust yourself when all men doubt you,
But make allowance for their doubting too;
If you can wait and not be tired of waiting,
Or being lied about, don't deal in lies,
Or being hated, don't give way to hating,
And yet don't look too good, nor talk too wise:

If you can dream – and not make dreams your master;
If you can think – and not make thoughts your aim;
If you can meet with Triumph and Disaster
And treat those two impostors just the same;
If you can bear to hear the truth you've spoken
Twisted by knaves to make a trap for fools,
Or watch the things you gave your life to, broken,
And stoop and build 'em up with worn-out tools:

If you can make one heap of all your winnings
And risk it on one turn of pitch-and-toss,
And lose, and start again at your beginnings
And never breathe a word about your loss;
If you can force your heart and nerve and sinew
To serve your turn long after they are gone,
And so hold on when there is nothing in you
Except the Will which says to them: 'Hold on!'

If you can talk with crowds and keep your virtue,
Or walk with Kings – nor lose the common touch,
If neither foes nor loving friends can hurt you,
If all men count with you, but none too much;
If you can fill the unforgiving minute
With sixty seconds' worth of distance run,
Yours is the Earth and everything that's in it,
And – which is more – you'll be a Man, my son!

Rudyard Kipling

Sir Smashum Uppe

Good afternoon, Sir Smashum Uppe!
We're having tea: do take a cup!
Sugar and milk? Now let me see –
Two lumps, I think? . . . Good gracious me!
The silly thing slipped off your knee!
Pray don't apologize, old chap:
A very trivial mishap!
So clumsy of you? How absurd!
My dear Sir Smashum, not a word!
Now do sit down and have another,
And tell us all about your brother –
You know, the one who broke his head.
Is the poor fellow still in bed?
A chair – allow me, sir! . . . Great Scott!
That *was* a nasty smash! Eh, what?
Oh, not at all: the chair was old –
Queen Anne, or so we have been told.
We've got at least a dozen more:
Just leave the pieces on the floor.
I want you to admire our view:
Come nearer to the window, do;
And look how beautiful . . . Tut, tut!
You didn't see that it was shut?

I hope you are not badly cut!
Not hurt? A fortunate escape!
Amazing! Not a single scrape!
And now, if you have finished tea,
I fancy you might like to see
A little thing or two I've got.
That china plate? Yes, worth a lot:
A beauty too . . . Ah, there it goes!
I trust it didn't hurt your toes?
Your elbow brushed it off the shelf?
Of course: I've done the same myself.
And now, my dear Sir Smashum – Oh,
You surely don't intend to go?
You *must* be off? Well, come again,
So glad you're fond of porcelain.

E.V. Rieu

October Tuesday

One crow in a high wind over Chelsea,
black against a rain sky loops and swings,
writes, '*Black against a rain sky*' with its wings.
One leaf, blown yellowing upward over Paultons Square,
writes '*Winter soon, yes, winter*' on the air.

Russell Hoban

The Word Party

Loving words clutch crimson roses,
Rude words sniff and pick their noses,
Sly words come dressed up as foxes,
Short words stand on cardboard boxes,
Common words tell jokes and gabble,
Complicated words play Scrabble,
Swear words stamp around and shout,
Hard words stare each other out,
Foreign words look lost and shrug,
Careless words trip on the rug,
Long words slouch with stooping shoulders,
Code words carry secret folders,
Silly words flick rubber bands,
Hyphenated words hold hands,
Strong words show off, bending metal,
Sweet words call each other 'petal',
Small words yawn and suck their thumbs
Till at last the morning comes.
Kind words give out farewell posies . . .

Snap! The dictionary closes.

Richard Edwards

In Grandma's Kitchen

She lets me chop
mint leaves to make
mint sauce: I do it so fine –
chop, chop on the breadboard –
we end up with a sort of
delicious green mud;

and she lets me peel
and core bramleys for apple pies:
sometimes I trim the pastry –
trim, trim with a bright knife –
then edge it round with a neat
fork so it looks like a small
bird's been walking the rim;

then I stir the custard
yellower and yellower;
and grandad comes in smiling
from the garden – it's a nice
slow Sunday; Blackie wags
his Sunday-best tail
and we all tuck in.

Matt Simpson

La Belle Dame sans Merci

O, what can ail thee, knight at arms,
  Alone and palely loitering?
The sedge has withered from the lake,
  And no birds sing.

O, what can ail thee, knight at arms,
  So haggard and so woe-begone?
The squirrel's granary is full,
  And the harvest's done.

I see a lily on thy brow
  With anguish moist and fever-dew,
And on thy cheeks a fading rose
  Fast withereth too.

I met a lady in the meads,
  Full beautiful – a faery's child,
Her hair was long, her foot was light,
  And her eyes were wild.

I made a garland for her head,
    And bracelets too, and fragrant zone,
She looked at me as she did love,
    And made sweet moan.

I set her on my pacing steed
    And nothing else saw all day long;
For sideways would she lean, and sing
    A faery's song.

She found me roots of relish sweet,
    And honey wild and manna dew;
And sure in language strange she said –
    I love thee true.

She took me to her elfin grot,
    And there she gazed and sighed full sore:
And there I shut her wild, wild eyes
    With kisses four.

And there she lullèd me asleep,
    And there I dreamed, ah woe betide,
The latest dream I ever dreamed
    On a cold hill side.

I saw pale kings and princes too,
    Pale warriors, death-pale were they all:
They cry'd – 'La Belle Dame sans Merci
    Hath thee in thrall!'

I saw their starved lips in the gloom
  With horrid warning gapèd wide,
And I awoke, and found me here
  On the cold hill side.

And this is why I sojourn here
  Alone and palely loitering,
Though the sedge is withered from the lake,
  And no birds sing.

John Keats

The Spare Room

It was just the spare room
the nobody-there room
the spooks-in-the-air room
the unbearable spare room.

It wasn't the guest room
the four-poster best room
the designed-to-impress room
the unusable guest room.

It wasn't the main room
the homely and plain room
the flop-on-the-bed room
Mum and Dad's own room.

It wasn't the blue room
the sweet lulla-loo room
the creep-on-your-feet room
the baby's asleep room.

It wasn't the bright room
the clothes-everywhere room
the music-all-night room
sister's scattered-about room.

It was just the spare room
the nobody-there room
the spooks-in-the-air room
the unbearable spare room.

Diana Hendry

Moonlit Apples

At the top of the house the apples are laid in rows,
And the skylight lets the moonlight in, and those
Apples are deep-sea apples of green. There goes
   A cloud on the moon in the autumn night.

A mouse in the wainscot scratches, and scratches, and then
There is no sound at the top of the house of men
Or mice; and the cloud is blown, and the moon again
   Dapples the apples with deep-sea light.

They are lying in rows there, under the gloomy beams;
On the sagging floor; they gather the silver streams
Out of the moon, those moonlit apples of dreams,
   And quiet is the steep stair under.

In the corridors under there is nothing but sleep.
And stiller than ever on orchard boughs they keep
Tryst with the moon, and deep is the silence, deep
   On the moon-washed apples of wonder.

John Drinkwater

Sharp Freckles
(for Ben Simmons)

He picks me up, his big thumbs under my armpits tickle,
then puts me down. On his belt there is a shining silver
  buckle.
I hold his hand and see, close up, the dark hairs on his
  knuckles.

He sings to me. His voice is loud and funny and I giggle.
Now we will eat. I listen to my breakfast as it crackles.
He nods and smiles. His eyes are birds in little nests of
  wrinkles.

We kick a ball, red and white, between us. When he tackles
I'm on the ground, breathing a world of grass. It prickles.
He bends. He lifts me high above his head. Frightened, I
  wriggle.

Face to his face, I watch the sweat above each caterpillar
  eyebrow trickle.
He rubs his nose on mine, once, twice, three times, and we
  both chuckle.
He hasn't shaved today. He kisses me. He has sharp
  freckles.

Carol Ann Duffy

Breakfast for One

Hot thick crusty buttery toast
Buttery toasty thick hot crust
Crusty buttery hot thick toast
Crusty thick hot toasty butter
Thick hot buttery crusty toast
Toasty buttery hot thick crust
Hot buttery thick crusty toast –

With marmalade is how I like it most!

Judith Nicholls

Sonnet 116

Let me not to the marriage of true minds
Admit impediments. Love is not love
Which alters when it alteration finds,
Or bends with the remover to remove:
O, no! it is an ever-fixèd mark,
That looks on tempests and is never shaken;
It is the star to every wandering bark,
Whose worth's unknown, although his height be taken.
Love's not Time's fool, though rosy lips and cheeks
Within his bending sickle's compass come;
Love alters not with his brief hours and weeks,
But bears it out even to the edge of doom.
    If this be error and upon me proved,
    I never writ, nor no man ever loved.

William Shakespeare

Ettykett

My mother knew a lot about manners,
  she said you should never slurp;
you should hold your saucer firmly,
  and not clang your teeth on the curp.

My father knew nothing of manners,
  all he could do was slurp;
and when I can't find a rhyming word,
  I set about making them urp.

John Rice

Sent a Letter to my Love

She wrote him a letter,
She wrote to her love,
She slipped her wee love-letter
Under her glove.

It had seventeen darlings,
And thirty-one dears,
And fifty-nine kisses,
And one or two tears.

She went to the pillar-box
Meaning to post it,
And when she arrived there,
Good gracious! she'd lost it!

And someone or other,
But who she can't prove,
Has picked up the letter
She wrote to her love.

If the butcher or baker
Or milkman or sweep
Has laughed at her letter
For shame she will weep.

Suppose all those darlings
And dears go amiss?
Suppose someone's stolen
A tear or a kiss?

It's as cruel as caging
A soft-breasted dove
To keep back the letter
She wrote to her love.

Eleanor Farjeon

Moon

'The moon is thousands of miles away,'
My uncle Trevor said.
Why can't he see
It's caught in a tree
Above our onion bed?

Gareth Owen

Beautiful Soup

Beautiful Soup, so rich and green,
    Waiting in a hot tureen!
Who for such dainties would not stoop?
Soup of the evening, beautiful Soup!
Soup of the evening, beautiful Soup!
    Beau-ootiful Soo-oop!
    Beau-ootiful Soo-oop!
Soo-oop of the e-e-evening,
    Beautiful, beautiful Soup!

Beautiful Soup! Who cares for fish,
    Game, or any other dish?
Who would not give all else for two p-
ennyworth only of beautiful Soup?
Pennyworth only of beautiful Soup?
    Beau-ootiful Soo-oop!
    Beau-ootiful Soo-oop!
Soo-oop of the e-e-evening,
    Beautiful, beauti-FUL SOUP!

Lewis Carroll

Purple Shoes

Mum and me had a row yesterday,
a big, exploding
howdareyouspeaktomelikethatI'mofftostayatGran's
kind of row.

It was about shoes.
I'd seen a pair of purple ones at Carter's,
heels not too high, soft suede, silver buckles;
'No,' she said.
'Not suitable for school.
I can't afford to buy rubbish.'
That's when we had our row.
I went to bed longing for those shoes.
They made footsteps in my mind,
kicking up dance dust;
I wore them in my dreams across a shiny floor,
under flashing coloured lights.
It was ruining my life not to have them.

This morning they were mine.
Mum relented and gave me the money.
I walked out of the store wearing new purple shoes.
I kept seeing myself reflected in shop windows
with purple shoes on,
walking to the bus stop,
walking the whole length of our street
wearing purple shoes.

On Monday I shall go to school in purple shoes.
Mum will say no a thousand furious times
But I don't care.
I'm not going to give in.

Irene Rawnsley

Ten Things Found in a Wizard's Pocket

A dark night.
Some words that nobody could ever spell.
A glass of water full to the top.
A large elephant.
A vest made from spiders' webs.
A handkerchief the size of a car park.
A bill from the wand shop.
A bucket full of stars and planets, to mix with the dark
   night.
A bag of magic mints you can suck for ever.
A snoring rabbit.

Ian McMillan

The Road Not Taken

Two roads diverged in a yellow wood,
And sorry I could not travel both
And be one traveller, long I stood
And looked down one as far as I could
To where it bent in the undergrowth;

Then took the other, as just as fair,
And having perhaps the better claim,
Because it was grassy and wanted wear;
Though as for that the passing there
Had worn them really about the same,

And both that morning equally lay
In leaves no step had trodden black.
Oh, I kept the first for another day!
Yet knowing how way leads on to way,
I doubted if I should ever come back.

I shall be telling this with a sigh
Somewhere ages and ages hence:
Two roads diverged in a wood, and I –
I took the one less travelled by,
And that has made all the difference.

Robert Frost.

Puma

Last night last night
I had a fright
I thought I saw a puma

Today today
it was all okay
I'd only seen a rumour

Trevor Millum

An Irish Airman Foresees His Death

I know that I shall meet my fate
Somewhere among the clouds above;
Those that I fight I do not hate,
Those that I guard I do not love;
My country is Kiltartan Cross,
My countrymen Kiltartan's poor,
No likely end could bring them loss
Or leave them happier than before.
Nor law, nor duty bade me fight,
Nor public men, nor cheering crowds,
A lonely impulse of delight
Drove to this tumult in the clouds;
I balanced all, brought all to mind,
The years to come seemed waste of breath,
A waste of breath the years behind
In balance with this life, this death.

W.B. Yeats

Dracula

After we'd climbed the many roads for Efori Nord
by bus past Bucharest, the capital of Romania,
I was dog tired. We went to a mountain room of pine,

and I searched the cupboards before I fell asleep.
That night I heard this weird flapping
at the window and woke up scared to death.

There, on the verandah, was a figure in black.
Casting no shadow. My hand instinctively flew
to my neck. Count Dracula was born here.

The cotton sheets were soaking with my sweat.
I could see his eyes flashing as he bent down;
imagine two small sinister holes in my skin.

If only we had stayed in Efori Nord,
playing ping-pong till kingdom come.
If only we hadn't come to the mountains.

I crawled along the pine floor to my father's bed.
It was empty. Just a white pillow and a headrest.
My dad gave a loud guffaw from the balcony.

Took off his black cape; threw back his head,
said, 'Got you going there, didn't I?
Okay. The joke's over. Back to your bed.'

Can you believe that? All I am asking is:
who needs an imagination, a fear, or a dread,
when what we've got is parents instead?

Jackie Kay

Fire, Burn; and Cauldron, Bubble

Round about the cauldron go;
In the poison'd entrails throw.
Toad, that under cold stone
Days and nights has thirty-one
Swelter'd venom, sleeping got,
Boil thou first i'th'charmed pot.
Double, double toil and trouble:
Fire, burn; and cauldron, bubble.
Fillet of a fenny snake,
In the cauldron boil and bake;
Eye of newt, and toe of frog,
Wool of bat, and tongue of dog,
Adder's fork, and blind-worm's sting,
Lizard's leg, and howlet's wing.
For a charm of powerful trouble,
Like a hell-broth boil and bubble.
Double, double toil and trouble:
Fire, burn; and cauldron, bubble.

William Shakespeare

Instructions for the last day in October

Leave the cottage at dusk.
Proceed to the sheep's skull
rammed on the gatepost.
Then plod the sodden field
where mists have gathered
to mutter like shawled hags.
Now enter the indigo wood.
Above, rooks will be cawing in
the coming night.
Note the trees' last leaves
hanging like withered hearts.
At the deep ditch's cauldron
crouch and feel the woodland cringe
in the grip of thistles.
Watch, watch spellbound,
as bubbles rise from the oily ooze
and know then you have arrived
    at
    Hallowe'en.

Wes Magee

November

Sheep in Winter

The sheep get up and make their many tracks
And bear a load of snow upon their backs,
And gnaw the frozen turnip to the ground
With sharp quick bite, and then go noising round
The boy that pecks the turnips all the day
And knocks his hands to keep the cold away
And laps his legs in straw to keep them warm
And hides behind the hedges from the storm.
The sheep, as tame as dogs, go where he goes
And try to shake their fleeces from the snows,
Then leave their frozen meal and wander round
The stubble stack that stands beside the ground,
And lie all night and face the drizzling storm
And shun the hovel where they might be warm.

John Clare

Camilla Caterpillar

Camilla Caterpillar kept a caterpillar killer-cat.
A caterpillar killer categorically she kept.
But alas the caterpillar killer-cat attacked Camilla
As Camilla Caterpillar catastrophically slept.

Mike Jubb

Perhaps
(To R.A.L. Died of Wounds in France, December 23rd, 1915)

Perhaps some day the sun will shine again,
   And I shall see that still the skies are blue,
And feel once more I do not live in vain,
   Although bereft of You.

November

Perhaps the golden meadows at my feet
  Will make the sunny hours of Spring seem gay,
And I shall find the white May blossoms sweet,
  Though You have passed away.

Perhaps the summer woods will shimmer bright,
  And crimson roses once again be fair,
And autumn harvest fields a rich delight,
  Although You are not there.

Perhaps some day I shall not shrink in pain
  To see the passing of the dying year,
And listen to the Christmas songs again,
  Although You cannot hear.

But, though kind Time may many joys renew,
  There is one greatest joy I shall not know
Again, because my heart for loss of You
  Was broken, long ago.

Vera Brittain

The Star

Twinkle, twinkle, little star,
How I wonder what you are!
Up above the world so high,
Like a diamond in the sky.

When the blazing sun is gone,
When he nothing shines upon,
Then you show your little light,
Twinkle, Twinkle, all the night.

Then the traveller in the dark,
Thanks you for your tiny spark,
He could not see which way to go,
If you did not twinkle so.

In the dark blue sky you keep,
And often through my curtains peep,
For you never shut your eye,
Till the sun is in the sky.

As your bright and tiny spark,
Lights the traveller in the dark –
Though I know not what you are,
Twinkle, twinkle, little star.

Jane Taylor

Remember, Remember

Remember, remember
The fifth of November:
Gunpowder, treason and plot.
I see no reason
Why gunpowder-treason
Should ever be forgot.

Anon.

Fireworks

They rise like sudden fiery flowers
   That burst upon the night,
Then fall to earth in burning showers
   Of crimson, blue, and white.

Like buds too wonderful to name,
   Each miracle unfolds,
And catherine-wheels begin to flame
   Like whirling marigolds.

Rockets and Roman candles make
   An orchard of the sky,
Whence magic trees their petals shake
   Upon each gazing eye.

                  James Reeves

On a Tired Housewife

Here lies a poor woman who was always tired,
She lived in a house where help wasn't hired:
Her last words on earth were: 'Dear friends, I am going
To where there's no cooking, or washing, or sewing,
For everything there is exact to my wishes,
For where they don't eat there's no washing of dishes.
I'll be where loud anthems will always be ringing,
But having no voice I'll be quit of the singing.
Don't mourn for me now, don't mourn for me never,
I am going to do nothing for ever and ever.'

Anon.

The New Computerized Timetable

Science will be in the Art Room.
Art in the History.
History in Maths.
And Maths in the swimming pool.

The lunch hour is from one o'clock to half-past,
Afternoon break has been moved to the morning.
Friday's timetable will operate
On alternate Thursdays.
Wednesday afternoon will be on Tuesday
Straight after Thursday's assembly.

From now on
We sit on desks
Write on chairs
And only wear hymn books when it's raining.

Next . . .
The new fire drill.

John Coldwell

from *The South Country*

If I ever become a rich man,
   Or if ever I grow to be old,
I will build a house with deep thatch,
   To shelter me from the cold,
And there shall the Sussex songs be sung
   And the story of Sussex told.

I will hold my house in the high wood
   Within a walk of the sea,
And the men that were boys when I was a boy
   Shall sit and drink with me.

Hilaire Belloc

Gray Goose and Gander

Gray goose and gander,
  Waft your wings together,
And carry the good king's daughter
  Over the one strand river.

Anon.

The Soldier

If I should die, think only this of me:
  That there's some corner of a foreign field
That is for ever England. There shall be
  In that rich earth a richer dust concealed;
A dust whom England bore, shaped, made aware,
  Gave, once, her flowers to love, her ways to roam,
A body of England's, breathing English air,
  Washed by the rivers, blest by suns of home.

And think, this heart, all evil shed away,
  A pulse in the eternal mind, no less
    Gives somewhere back the thoughts by
      England given;
Her sights and sounds; dreams happy as her day;
  And laughter, learnt of friends; and gentleness,
    In hearts at peace, under an English heaven.

Rupert Brooke

London Bells

Two sticks and an apple,
Ring the bells at Whitechapel.

Old Father Bald Pate,
Ring the bells Aldgate.

Maids in white aprons,
Ring the bells at St Catherine's.

Oranges and lemons,
Ring the bells at St Clement's.

When will you pay me?
Ring the bells at the Old Bailey.

When I am rich,
Ring the bells at Fleetditch.

When will that be?
Ring the bells at Stepney.

When I am old,
Ring the great bell at Paul's.

Anon.

My Mother Said

My mother said I never should
Play with the gypsies in the wood;
If I did, she would say,
Naughty girl to disobey.
Your hair shan't curl
And your shoes shan't shine,
You gypsy girl,
You shan't be mine.

And my father said that if I did
He'd rap my head with the tea-pot lid.
The wood was dark; the grass was green;
In came Sally with a tambourine.
I went to the sea – no ship to get across;
I paid ten shillings for a blind white horse;
I up on his back and was off in a crack,
Sally tell my mother I shall never come back.

Anon.

Jabberwocky

'Twas brillig, and the slithy toves
Did gyre and gimble in the wabe;
All mimsy were the borogoves,
And the mome raths outgrabe.

'Beware the Jabberwock, my son!
The jaws that bite, the claws that catch!
Beware the Jubjub bird, and shun
The frumious Bandersnatch!'

He took his vorpal sword in hand:
Long time the manxome foe he sought –
So rested he by the Tumtum tree,
And stood awhile in thought.

And as in uffish thought he stood,
The Jabberwock, with eyes of flame,
Came whiffling through the tulgey wood,
And burbled as it came!

One, two! One, two! And through and through
　　The vorpal blade went snicker-snack!
He left it dead, and with its head
　　　　He went galumphing back.

'And hast thou slain the Jabberwock?
　　Come to my arms, my beamish boy!
O frabjous day! Callooh! Callay!'
　　　　He chortled in his joy.

'Twas brillig, and the slithy toves
　　Did gyre and gimble in the wabe;
All mimsy were the borogoves,
　　　　And the mome raths outgrabe.

Lewis Carroll

The Smell of Chrysanthemums

The chestnut leaves are toasted. Conkers spill
Upon the pavements. Gold is vying with
Yellow, ochre, brown. There is a feel
Of dyings and departures. Smoky breath
  Rises and I know how Winter comes
  When I can smell the rich chrysanthemums.

It is so poignant and it makes me mourn
for what? The going year? The sun's eclipse?
All these and more. I see the dead leaves burn
And everywhere the Summer lies in heaps.
  I close my eyes and feel how Winter comes
  With acrid incense of chrysanthemums.

I shall not go to school again and yet
There's an old sadness that disturbs me most.
The nights come early; every bold sunset
Tells me that Autumn soon will be a ghost,
  But I know best how Winter always comes
  In the wide scent of strong chrysanthemums.

Elizabeth Jennings

The Sound Collector

A stranger called this morning
Dressed all in black and grey
Put every sound into a bag
And carried them away.

The whistling of the kettle
The turning of the lock
The purring of the kitten
The ticking of the clock

The popping of the toaster
The crunching of the flakes
When you spread the marmalade
The scraping noise it makes

The hissing of the frying-pan
The ticking of the grill
The bubbling of the bathtub
As it starts to fill

The drumming of the raindrops
On the window-pane
When you do the washing-up
The gurgle of the drain

The crying of the baby
The squeaking of the chair
The swishing of the curtain
The creaking of the stair

A stranger called this morning
He didn't leave his name
Left us only silence
Life will never be the same.

Roger McGough

Our Bonfire

Our bonfire still smoulders as we start back for home,
The blue woodsmoke floats straight to the sky
Wafting feathers of ash from the foot of the hollow
That's hidden from everyone's eye.

The heat on our cheeks! The spark and the spit!
The cracklings, the smart of the smoke! –
Dwindling down now to nothing, grey-gentle as down,
Where we snuggled our taties to cook.

The sun slides down, the long night will be cold,
But I'll think, when I'm tucked up in bed,
Of somebody sleeping, secret and warm, where today
Our rotten beechboughs blazed red.

Smoke in our nostrils, and smoke on our tongues,
Ash on our eyelids, our clothes and our hair –
As, smelling all kippered, we saunter to tea:
And trouble, but none of us care.

Brian Lee

I Had a Little Nut Tree

I had a little nut tree,
Nothing would it bear,
But a silver nutmeg,
And a golden pear.
The King of Spain's daughter,
Came to visit me,
And all was because of
My little nut tree.
I skipped over water
I danced over sea,
And all the birds in the air
Could not catch me.

Anon.

Bedtime

When I go upstairs to bed,
I usually give a loud cough.
This is to scare The Monster off.

When I come to my room,
I usually slam the door right back.
This is to squash The Man in Black
Who sometimes hides there.

Nor do I walk to the bed,
But usually run and jump instead.
This is to stop The Hand –
Which is under there all night –
From grabbing my ankles.

Allan Ahlberg

The Playground Monster

It grabbed me
with its tarmac jaws
and then it tried
to bite me.

It grasped me
with its gravelly paws
and then it tried
to fight me.

I live in fear of walking
across its great black back.

I think it knows I'm talking.
It listens at a crack!

I fear its greedy darkness,
the way it seems to need

to reach out when I'm running
and grab me for a feed.

It grabbed me
with its tarmac jaws
and then it tried
to bite me.

It grasped me
with its gravelly paws
and then it tried
to fight me.

Pie Corbett

Daisy

Daisy, Daisy,
Give me your answer do,
I'm half crazy
All for the love of you;
It won't be a stylish marriage,
For I can't afford a carriage –
But you'll look sweet
Upon the seat
Of a bicycle made for two!

Anon.

The Dragon in the Cellar

There's a dragon!
There's a dragon!
There's a dragon in the cellar!
Yeah, we've got a cellar-dweller.
There's a dragon in the cellar.

He's a cleanliness fanatic,
takes his trousers and his jacket
to the dragon in the attic
who puts powder by the packet
in a pre-set automatic
with a rattle and a racket
that's disturbing and dramatic.

There's a dragon!
There's a dragon!
There's a dragon in the cellar
with a flame that's red 'n' yeller.
There's a dragon in the cellar . . .

. . . and a dragon on the roof
who's only partly waterproof,
so she's borrowed an umbrella
from the dragon in the cellar.

There's a dragon!
There's a dragon!
There's a dragon in the cellar!
If you smell a panatella
it's the dragon in the cellar.

And the dragon from the study's
helping out his cellar buddy,
getting wet and soap-suddy
with the dragon from the loo
there to give a hand too,
while the dragon from the porch
supervises with a torch.
Though the dragon from the landing,
through a slight misunderstanding,
is busy paint-stripping and sanding.

There's a dragon!
There's a dragon!
There's a dragon in the cellar!
Find my dad, and tell the feller
there's a dragon in the cellar . . .

. . . where the dragon from my room
goes zoom, zoom, zoom
in a cloud of polish and spray-perfume,
cos he's the dragon whom
they pay to brighten up the gloom
with a mop and a duster and a broom, broom, broom.

There's a dragon!
There's a dragon!
There's a dragon in the cellar!
Gonna get my mum and tell her
there's a dragon in the cellar.

Nick Toczek

from *Auguries of Innocence*

To see a World in a Grain of Sand
And a Heaven in a Wild Flower,
Hold Infinity in the palm of your hand
And Eternity in an hour.

William Blake

Brother

I had a little brother
And I brought him to my mother
And I said I want another
Little brother for a change.
But she said don't be a bother
so I took him to my father
And I said this little bother
Of a brother's very strange.

But he said one little brother
Is exactly like another
And every little brother
Misbehaves a bit he said.
So I took the little brother
From my mother and my father
And I put the little bother
Of a brother back to bed.

Mary Ann Hoberman

A Birthday

My heart is like a singing bird,
   Whose nest is in a watered shoot;
My heart is like an apple-tree
   Whose boughs are bent with thick-set fruit;
My heart is like a rainbow shell
   That paddles in a halcyon sea;
My heart is gladder than all these
   Because my love is come to me.

Raise me a dais of silk and down;
   Hang it with vair and purple dyes;
Carve it in doves and pomegranates,
   And peacocks with a hundred eyes;
Work it in gold and silver grapes,
   In leaves and silver fleurs-de-lys;
Because the birthday of my life
   Is come, my love is come to me.

Christina Rossetti

Today I saw a little worm

Today I saw a little worm
Wriggling on his belly.
Perhaps he'd like to come inside
And see what's on the Telly.

Spike Milligan

Night Mail

This is the night mail crossing the border,
Bringing the cheque and the postal order,
Letters for the rich, letters for the poor,
The shop at the corner and the girl next door.
Pulling up Beattock, a steady climb –
The gradient's against her, but she's on time.

Past cotton grass and moorland boulder
Shovelling white steam over her shoulder,
Snorting noisily as she passes
Silent miles of wind-bent grasses.
Birds turn their heads as she approaches,
Stare from the bushes at her blank-faced coaches.
Sheepdogs cannot turn her course,
They slumber on with paws across.
In the farm she passes no one wakes,
But the jug in the bedroom gently shakes.

Dawn freshens, the climb is done.
Down towards Glasgow she descends
Towards the steam tugs yelping down the glade of cranes,
Towards the fields of apparatus, the furnaces
Set on the dark plain like gigantic chessmen.
All Scotland waits for her:
In the dark glens, beside the pale-green lochs
Men long for news.

Letters of thanks, letters from banks,
Letters of joy from girl and boy,
Receipted bills and invitations
To inspect new stock or visit relations,
And applications for situations
And timid lovers' declarations
And gossip, gossip from all the nations,
News circumstantial, news financial.

Letters with holiday snaps to enlarge in,
Letters with faces scrawled in the margin,
Letters from uncles, cousins and aunts,
Letters to Scotland from the South of France,
Letters of condolence to Highlands and Lowlands,
Notes from overseas to Hebrides –
Written on paper of every hue,
The pink, the violet, the white and the blue,
The chatty, the catty, the boring, adoring,
The cold and official and the heart's outpouring,
Clever, stupid, short and long,
The typed and the printed and the spelt all wrong.
Thousands are still asleep
Dreaming of terrifying monsters,
Of a friendly tea beside the band at Cranston's or
    Crawford's:
Asleep in working Glasgow, asleep in well-set Edinburgh,
Asleep in granite Aberdeen.
They continue their dreams;
But shall wake soon and long for letters,
And none will hear the postman's knock
Without a quickening of the heart,
For who can hear and feel himself forgotten?

W.H. Auden

The Microbe

The Microbe is so very small
You cannot make him out at all,
But many sanguine people hope
To see him through a microscope.
His jointed tongue that lies beneath
A hundred curious rows of teeth;
His seven tufted tails with lots
Of lovely pink and purple spots,
On each of which a pattern stands,
Composed of forty separate bands;
His eyebrows of a tender green;
All these have never yet been seen –
But Scientists, who ought to know,
Assure us that they must be so . . .
Oh! let us never, never doubt
What nobody is sure about!

Hilaire Belloc

The Furry Ones

I like –
the furry ones –
the waggy ones
the purry ones
the hoppy ones
that hurry,

The glossy ones
the saucy ones
the sleepy ones
the leapy ones
the mousy ones
that scurry,

The snuggly ones
the huggly ones
the never, never
ugly ones . . .
all soft
and warm
and furry.

Aileen Fisher

Things to Remember

The buttercups in May,
The wild rose on the spray,
The poppy in the hay,

The primrose in the dell,
The freckled foxglove bell,
The honeysuckle's smell

Are things I would remember
When cheerless, raw November
Makes room for dark December.

James Reeves

December

Footballers in the Park

December. Wet Saturday in the park.
It's late afternoon and it's growing dark

as a bevy of boys play their football game.
Most wear baggy shorts. One goalie's lame.

Posts are old jerseys and hand-me-down coats;
the boys' boots are bulky as rowing boats.

Leather ball's sodden and heavy with mud.
It thumps a boy's face with a squelchy thud

and blood dribbles down from a nose struck numb:
a fat lad stunningly skids on his bum.

December

One boy shivers in his 'Wednesday' shirt,
the collar's ripped and he's plastered with dirt.

The game rattles on; chill drizzle sets in.
The wind in the trees makes a Cup Final din.

Distantly, lights shine on the wet street
unnoticed by boys whose thundering feet

are playing the game. But the hour grows late.
Here comes the park keeper to padlock the gate.

And the year is 1948.

Wes Magee

The Runaway

Once when the snow of the year was beginning to fall,
We stopped by a mountain pasture to say, 'Whose colt?'
A little Morgan had one forefoot on the wall,
The other curled at his breast. He dipped his head
And snorted at us. And then he had to bolt.
We heard the miniature thunder where he fled,
And we saw him, or thought we saw him, dim and grey,
Like a shadow against the curtain of falling flakes.
'I think the little fellow's afraid of the snow.
He isn't winter-broken. It isn't play
With the little fellow at all. He's running away.
I doubt if even his mother could tell him, "Sakes,
It's only weather." He'd think she didn't know!
Where is his mother? He can't be out alone.'
And now he comes again with clatter of stone,
And mounts the wall again with whited eyes
And all his tail that isn't hair up straight.
He shudders his coat as if to throw off flies.
'Whoever it is that leaves him out so late,
When other creatures have gone to stall and bin,
Ought to be told to come and take him in.'

Robert Frost

Mr McGuire

Old Mr McGuire, blind as a bat,
had a rabbit, a weasel, a dog and a cat.
He stroked them all as he sat by the fire,
some days they felt smooth,
and some days like wire.
With a bark, a hiss, a squeak and miaow
they demanded attention
and all got it somehow.
Old Mr McGuire, he loved them all –
'To me you're one creature
you're all from the same sack.
God brought you here
and he'll take you back.
You may think you're different
but, heavens above –
you are all of you loved
with one single love.'

Brian Patten

Batman

Batman
Age 10½
Patrols the streets of his suburb
At night
Between 7 and 8 o'clock,
If he is out later than this
he is spanked
and sent to bed
Without supper.

Batman
Almost 11
Patrols the streets of his suburb
At night
After he has finished his homework.

Batman,
His freckles
And secret identity
Protected
By the mask and cloak
His Auntie Elsie
Made on her sewing machine,
Patrols
At night
Righting Wrongs.

Tonight he is on the trail of
Raymond age 11
(large for his age)
Who has stolen Stephen's
Gobstoppers and football cards.

Batman
Patrolling the streets of his suburb
Righting Wrongs
Finds Raymond,
Demands the return of the stolen goods.
Raymond knocks him over,
Rips his mask,
Tears his cloak,
And steals his utility belt.
Batman starts to cry,
Wipes his eyes with his cape
(His hankie was in the belt).

Next day
Auntie Elsie says
This is the 14th time
I've had to mend your
Batman costume
If it happens again
You'll have to whistle for it.

Batman
Eats a bag of crisps.

John Turner

The Fallow Deer at the Lonely House

One without looks in tonight
  Through the curtain-chink
From the sheet of glistening white;
One without looks in tonight
  As we sit and think
  By the fender-brink.

We do not discern those eyes
   Watching in the snow;
Lit by lamps of rosy dyes
We do not discern those eyes
   Wondering, aglow,
    Fourfooted, tiptoe.

Thomas Hardy

I Think my Teacher is a Cowboy

It's not just
That she rides to school on a horse
And carries a Colt 45 in her handbag.

It's not just
the way she walks;
hands hanging over her hips.

It's not just
the way she dresses;
stetson hat and spurs on her boots.

It's not just the way she talks;
calling the playground the corral,
    the Head's room the Sheriff's office,
    the school canteen the chuck wagon,
    the school bus the stagecoach,
    the bike sheds the livery stable.

What gives her away
Is when the hometime pips go.
She slaps her thigh
And cries
'Yee ha!'

John Coldwell

All the world's a stage

All the world's a stage,
And all the men and women merely players:
They have their exits and their entrances;
And one man in his time plays many parts,
His acts being seven ages. At first the infant,
Mewling and puking in the nurse's arms.
And then the whining schoolboy, with his satchel,
And shining morning face, creeping like snail
Unwillingly to school. And then the lover,
Sighing like furnace, with a woeful ballad
Made to his mistress' eyebrow. Then a soldier,
Full of strange oaths, and bearded like the pard,
Jealous in honour, sudden and quick in quarrel,
Seeking the bubble reputation
Even in the cannon's mouth. And then the justice,
In fair round belly with good capon lin'd,
With eyes severe, and beard of formal cut,
Full of wise saws and modern instances;
And so he plays his part. The sixth age shifts
Into the lean and slipper'd pantaloon,
With spectacles on nose and pouch on side,
His youthful hose well sav'd, a world too wide
For his shrunk shank; and his big manly voice,

Turning again toward childish treble, pipes
And whistles in his sound. Last scene of all,
That ends this strange eventful history,
Is second childishness and mere oblivion,
Sans teeth, sans eyes, sans taste, sans everything.

William Shakespeare

The Garden's Full of Witches

Mum! The garden's full of witches!
Come quick and see the witches.
  There's a full moon out,
  And they're flying about,
Come on! You'll miss the witches.

Oh Mum! You're missing the witches.
You have never seen so many witches.
  They're casting spells!
  There are horrible smells!
Come on! You'll miss the witches.

Mum, hurry! Come look at the witches.
The shrubbery's bursting with witches.
   They've turned our Joan
   Into a garden gnome.
Come on! You'll miss the witches.

Oh no! You'll miss the witches.
The garden's black with witches.
   Come on! Come on!
   Too late! They've gone.
Oh, you always miss the witches!

Colin McNaughton

Snowball

I made myself a snowball
As perfect as could be.
I thought I'd keep it as a pet
And let it sleep with me.
I made it some pajamas
And a pillow for its head.
Then last night it ran away,
But first – it wet the bed.

Shel Silverstein

Twinkle, Twinkle, Little Bat

Twinkle, twinkle, little bat!
How I wonder what you're at!
Up above the world you fly,
Like a tea-tray in the sky.
Twinkle, twinkle –
Twinkle, twinkle, twinkle, twinkle.

Lewis Carroll

Snow and Snow

Snow is sometimes a she, a soft one.
Her kiss on your cheek, her finger on your sleeve
In early December, on a warm evening,
And you turn to meet her, saying 'It's snowing!'
But it is not. And nobody's there.
Empty and calm is the air.

December

Sometimes the snow is a he, a sly one.
  Weakly he signs the dry stone with a damp spot.
Waifish he floats and touches the pond and is not.
  Treacherous-beggarly he falters, and taps at the window.
    A little longer he clings to the grass-blade tip
    Getting his grip.

Then how she leans, how furry foxwrap she nestles
  The sky with her warm, and the earth with her softness.
How her lit crowding fairytales sink through the space-
  silence
  To build her palace, till it twinkles in starlight –
    Too frail for a foot
    Or a crumb of soot.

Then how his muffled armies move in all night
  And we wake and every road is blockaded
Every hill taken and every farm occupied
  And the white glare of his tents is on the ceiling.
    And all that dull blue day and on into the gloaming
    We have to watch more coming.

Then everything in the rubbish-heaped world
  Is a bridesmaid at her miracle.
Dunghills and crumbly dark old barns are bowed in the
  chapel of her sparkle,
  The gruesome boggy cellars of the wood
    Are a wedding of lace
    Now taking place.

Ted Hughes

The Reverend Sabine Baring-Gould

The Reverend Sabine Baring-Gould,
    Rector (sometime) at Lew,
Once at a Christmas party asked,
    'Whose pretty child are you?'

(The Rector's family was long,
    His memory was poor,
And as to who was who had grown
    Increasingly unsure.)

At this, the infant on the stair
    Most sorrowfully sighed.
'Whose pretty little girl am I?
    Why, *yours*, papa!' she cried.

Charles Causley

Angels

We are made from light.
Called into being we burn
Brighter than the silver white
Of hot magnesium.
More sudden than yellow phosphorous.
We are the fire of heaven;
Blue flames and golden ether.

We are from stars.
Spinning beyond the farthest galaxy
In an instant gathered to this point
We shine, speak our messages and go,
Back to the brilliance.
We are not separate, not individual,
We are what we are made of. Only
Shaped sometimes into tall-winged warriors,
Our faces solemn as swords,
Our voices joy.

The skies are cold;
Suns do not warm us;
Fire does not burn itself.
Only once we touched you
And felt a human heat.
Once, in the brightness of the frost,
Above the hills, in glittering starlight,
Once, we sang.

Jan Dean

Just Doing My Job

I'm one of Herod's Henchmen.
We don't have much to say,
We just charge through the audience
In a Henchman sort of way.

We all wear woolly helmets
To hide our hair and ears,
And Wellingtons sprayed silver
To match our tinfoil spears.

Our swords are made of cardboard
So blood will not be spilled
If we trip and stab a parent
When the hall's completely filled.

We don't look *very* scary,
We're mostly small and shy,
And some of us wear glasses,
But we give the thing a try.

We whisper Henchman noises
While Herod hunts for strangers,
And then we all charge out again
Like nervous Power Rangers.

Yet when the play is over
And Miss is out of breath
We'll charge like Henchmen through the hall
And scare our mums to death.

Clare Bevan

I Saw Three Ships

I saw three ships come sailing in,
Come sailing in, come sailing in;
I saw three ships come sailing in,
On Christmas Day in the morning.

And what was in those ships all three,
Those ships all three, those ships all three?
And what was in those ships all three,
On Christmas Day in the morning?

Our Saviour Christ and his lady,
And his lady, and his lady;
Our Saviour Christ and his lady,
On Christmas Day in the morning.

Anon.

Christmas at Four Winds Farm

With the tambourine tinkle of ice on the moor
and the winter moon white as a bone,
my grandad and his father
set out to bring Christmas home.

A wild winter wizard had grizzled the gorse
and spangled the splinter-sharp leaves,
when the light of their wind-swinging lantern
found a magical Christmas tree.

From the glittering town at the end of the dale
the carols grew sweeter and bolder,
as my grandad's smiling father
carried Christmas home on his shoulder.

Maureen Haselhurst

Christmas Market

Tall, white-haired in her widow's black,
My Nanna took me, balaclava'd from the cold,
To where stalls shimmered in a splash of gold,
Buttery light from wind-twitched lamps and all
The Christmas hoards were heaped above my eyes,
A shrill cascade of tinsel set to fall
In a sea of shivering colours on the frosty
Foot-pocked earth. I smelt the roasted nuts,
Drank heavy sarsaparilla in thick glasses far
Too hot to hold and chewed a liquorice root
That turned into a soggy yellow brush. The man
Who wound the barrel-organ let me turn
The handle and I jangled out a tune –
And 'Lily of Laguna' spangled out into the still night air
To go on spinning through the turning years.

Then we walked home. I clutched a bright tin car
With half-men painted on the windows, chewed a sweet
And held my Nanna's hand as she warmed mine,
One glove lost turning out the clattering music.
And I looked up at the circus of the stars
That spread across the city and our street
Coated with a Christmas-cake layer of frost,
And nobody under all those stars I thought
Was a half of a half of a half as happy as me.

Mike Harding

Snow

Feathery soft and quiet the snow;
It covers the road
    and the walk
    and the rooftops
    and whispers to the world:
Shhh!

Margaret R. Moore

We Are Not Alone

Captain's Log. Starship Saturnalian.
Earth year 2030, day 358 –
The new drive worked! We've tracked the alien
spacecraft that vanished from earth's orbit late

last night. We followed its fantastic leap
across the galaxy and now can see
its sledge-like shape dropping in steep
descent to a planet. Incredibly

a single cosmonaut whose suit glows red
clings to its tail and holds long ropes to steer
a group of prancing creatures: from each head
sprout aerials that make them look like deer.

The planet's steaming, its surface smooth and
dark as Christmas pudding. Prepare to land!

Dave Calder

Carol of the Signs

Whiter than silver shines
Last night's fallen snow,
It is thick with signs,
Yet I saw none go.

Naked feet, three pair,
Left prints upon the snow,
Because the feet were bare,
Poor men's feet, I know.

Wheels of chariots rolled
Last night across the snow,
Great men in the cold
Rode before cockcrow.

Lo! A newborn lamb
Ran on the fallen snow,
By his side his dam
Gently trod and slow.

Here a Cross was laid
Heavy on the snow,
Somebody here stayed
To rest a moment so.

And here, the brightest scar
Of all upon the snow,
The imprint of a Star,
A heavenly Star, dropped low.

Thick as dew on grass
Lie signs upon the snow,
Yet I heard none pass,
And I saw none go.

Eleanor Farjeon

The First Tree in the Greenwood

Now the holly bears a berry as white as the milk,
And Mary bore Jesus, who was wrapped up in silk:
   And Mary bore Jesus Christ,
   Our Saviour for to be,
   And the first tree in the greenwood, it was the holly.

Now the holly bears a berry as green as the grass,
And Mary bore Jesus, who died on the cross:
   And Mary bore Jesus Christ,
   Our Saviour for to be,
   And the first tree in the greenwood, it was the holly.

Now the holly bears a berry as black as the coal,
And Mary bore Jesus, who died for us all:
   And Mary bore Jesus Christ,
   Our Saviour for to be,
   And the first tree in the greenwood, it was the holly.

Now the holly bears a berry, as blood is it red,
Then trust we our Saviour, who rose from the dead:
   And Mary bore Jesus Christ,
   Our Saviour for to be,
   And the first tree in the greenwood, it was the holly.

Anon.

What the Donkey Saw

No room in the inn, of course,
And not that much in the stable,
What with the shepherds, Magi, Mary,
Joseph, the heavenly host –
Not to mention the baby
Using our manger as a cot.
You couldn't have squeezed another cherub in
For love or money.

Still, in spite of the overcrowding,
I did my best to make them feel wanted.
I could see the baby and I
would be going places together.

U.A. Fanthorpe

Christmas is Coming

Christmas is coming,
   The geese are getting fat,
Please to put a penny
   In the old man's hat.
If you haven't got a penny,
   A ha'penny will do;
If you haven't got a ha'penny,
   Then God bless you!

Anon.

A Visit From St Nicholas

'Twas the night before Christmas, when all through the
house
Not a creature was stirring, not even a mouse;
The stockings were hung by the chimney with care,
In hopes that St Nicholas soon would be there;
The children were nestled all snug in their beds,
While visions of sugar-plums danced in their heads;
And mamma in her 'kerchief, and I in my cap,
Had just settled our brains for a long winter's nap –
When out on the lawn there arose such a clatter,
I sprang from my bed to see what was the matter.
Away to the window I flew like a flash,
Tore open the shutters, and threw up the sash.
The moon, on the breast of the new-fallen snow,
Gave the lustre of midday to objects below;
When, what to my wondering eyes should appear,
But a miniature sleigh and eight tiny reindeer,
With a little old driver, so lively and quick,
I knew in a moment it must be St Nick.
More rapid than eagles his coursers they came,
And he whistled, and shouted, and called them by name:
'Now, *Dasher*! now, *Dancer*! now, *Prancer* and *Vixen*!
On, *Comet*! on, *Cupid*! on, *Donder* and *Blitzen*!

To the top of the porch! to the top of the wall!
Now dash away! dash away! dash away all!'
As dry leaves that before the wild hurricane fly,
When they meet with an obstacle, mount to the sky;
So up to the house-top the coursers they flew
With the sleigh full of toys, and St Nicholas too.
And then, in a twinkling, I heard on the roof
The prancing and pawing of each little hoof –
As I drew in my head, and was turning around,
Down the chimney St Nicholas came with a bound.
He was dressed all in fur, from his head to his foot,
And his clothes were all tarnished with ashes and soot;
A bundle of toys he had flung on his back,
And he looked like a pedlar just opening his pack.
His eyes – how they twinkled; his dimples, how merry!
His cheeks were like roses, his nose like a cherry!
His droll little mouth was drawn up like a bow,
And the beard of his chin was as white as the snow;
The stump of a pipe he held tight in his teeth,
And the smoke it encircled his head like a wreath;
He had a broad face and a little round belly
That shook, when he laughed, like a bowl full of jelly.
He was chubby and plump, a right jolly old elf,
And I laughed when I saw him, in spite of myself;
A wink of his eye and a twist of his head
Soon gave me to know I had nothing to dread;
He spoke not a word, but went straight to his work,
And filled all the stockings; then turned with a jerk,
And laying his fingers aside of his nose,

And giving a nod, up the chimney he rose;
He sprang to his sleigh, to his team gave a whistle,
And away they all flew like the down of a thistle.
But I heard him exclaim, ere he drove out of sight,
'Happy Christmas to all, and to all a good night!'

Clement Clarke Moore

O Little Town

O little town of Bethlehem
  How still we see thee lie!
Above thy deep and dreamless sleep
  The silent stars go by.
Yet in thy dark streets shineth
  The everlasting light;
The hopes and fears of all the years
  Are met in thee tonight.

O morning stars, together
   Proclaim the holy birth,
And praises sing to God the King,
   And peace to men on earth;
For Christ is born of Mary;
   And, gathered all above,
While mortals sleep, the angels keep
   Their watch of wondering love.

How silently, how silently,
   The wondrous gift is given!
So God imparts to human hearts
   The blessings of his heaven.
No ear may hear his coming;
   But in this world of sin,
Where meek souls will receive him, still
   The dear Christ enters in.

Where children pure and happy
   Pray to the blessèd Child,
Where misery cries out to thee,
   Son of the mother mild:
Where charity stands watching
   And faith holds wide the door,
The dark night wakes, the glory breaks,
   And Christmas comes once more.

O holy Child of Bethlehem,
   Descend to us, we pray;
Cast out our sin, and enter in,
   Be born in us today.
We hear the Christmas Angels
   The great glad tidings tell:
O come to us, abide with us,
   Our Lord Emmanuel.

Bishop Phillips Brooks

Nothingmas Day

No it wasn't.

It was Nothingmas Day and all the children in Notown were not tingling with excitement as they lay unawake in their heaps.
D
  o
    w
      n
        s
          t
            a
              r
                s their parents were busily not placing the last crackermugs, glimmerslips and sweetlumps on the Nothingmas Tree.

Hey! But what was that invisible trail of chummy sparks or vaulting stars across the sky?

Father Nothingmas – drawn by 18 or 21 rainmaidens!

Father Nothingmas – his sackbut bulging with air!

Father Nothingmas – was not on his way!

(From the streets of the snowless town came the quiet of unsung carols and the merry silence of the steeple bell.)

Next morning the children did not fountain out of bed with cries of WHOOPERATION! They picked up their Nothingmas Stockings and with traditional quiperamas such as: 'Look what I haven't got! It's just what I didn't want!' pulled their stockings on their ordinary legs.

For breakfast they ate – breakfast.

Afterwards they all avoided the Nothingmas Tree, where Daddy, his face failing to beam like a leaky torch, was not distributing gemgames, sodaguns, golly-trolleys, jars of humdrums and packets of slubberated croakers.

Off, off, off went the children to school, soaking each other with no howls of 'Merry Nothingmas and a Happy No Year!', and not pulping each other with no-balls.

At school Miss Whatnot taught them to write No Thank You Letters.

Home they burrowed for Nothingmas Dinner.
The table was not groaning under all manner of

No Turkey
No Spiced Ham
No Sprouts
No Cranberry Jellysauce
No Not Nowt

There was not one shoot of glee as the Nothingmas
Pudding, unlit, was not brought in. Mince pies were not
available, nor was there any demand for them.

Then, as another Nothingmas clobbered to a close, they all
haggled off to bed where they slept happily never after.

and that is not the end of the story . . .

Adrian Mitchell

Telling

One, two, three, four,
Telling Miss that Gary swore.
Five, six, seven, eight,
Now I haven't got a mate.

Wendy Cope

The Day After The Day After Boxing Day

On the day after the day after Boxing Day
Santa wakes up, eventually,
puts away his big red suit and wellies,
lets Rudolph and the gang out into the meadow
then shaves his head and beard.

He puts on his new cool sunglasses,
baggy blue Bermuda shorts (he's sick of red),
yellow stripy T-shirt that doesn't quite cover his belly
and lets his toes breathe in flip-flops.

Packing a bucket and spade,
fifteen tubes of Factor Twenty suncream
and seventeen romantic novels
he fills his Walkman with the latest sounds,
is glad to use a proper suitcase instead of the old sack
and heads off into the Mediterranean sunrise
enjoying the comforts of a Boeing 747
(although he passes on the free drinks).

Six months later,
relaxed, red and a little more than stubbly,
he looks at his watch, adjusts his wide-brimmed sunhat,
mops the sweat from his brow and strokes his chin,
wondering why holidays always seem to go so quickly.

Paul Cookson

A Child's Calendar

No visitors in January.
A snowman smokes a cold pipe in the yard.

They stand about like ancient women,
The February hills.
They have seen many a coming and going, the hills.

In March Moorfea is littered
With knock-kneed lambs.

Daffodils at the door in April,
Three shawled Marys.
A lark splurges in galilees of sky.

And in May
A russet stallion shoulders the hill apart.
The mares tremble.

The June bee
Bumps in the pane with a heavy bag of plunder.

December

Strangers swarm in July
With cameras, binoculars, bird books.

He thumped the crag in August,
A blind blue whale.

September crofts get wrecked in blond surges.
They struggle, the harvesters.
They drag loaf and ale-kirn into winter.

In October the fishmonger
Argues, pleads, threatens at the shore.

Nothing in November
But tinkers at the door, keening, with cans.

Some December midnight
Christ, lord, lie warm in our byre.
Here are stars, an ox, poverty enough.

George Mackay Brown

The Land of Counterpane

When I was sick and lay a-bed,
I had two pillows at my head,
And all my toys beside me lay
To keep me happy all the day.

And sometimes for an hour or so
I watched my leaden soldiers go,
With different uniforms and drills,
Among the bed-clothes, through the hills;

And sometimes sent my ships in fleets
All up and down among the sheets;
Or brought my trees and houses out,
And planted cities all about.

I was the giant great and still
That sits upon the pillow-hill,
And sees before him, dale and plain,
The pleasant land of counterpane.

Robert Louis Stevenson

Auld Lang Syne

Should auld acquaintance be forgot,
And never brought to min'?
Should auld acquaintance be forgot,
And auld lang syne?

    For auld lang syne, my dear.
    For auld lang syne,
    We'll tak a cup o' kindness yet,
    For auld lang syne.

We twa hae run about the braes,
And pu'd the gowans fine;
But we've wandered mony a weary foot
Sin' auld lang syne.
We twa hae paidled i' the burn,
From morning sun till dine;
But seas between us braid hae roared
Sin' auld lang syne.

And there's a hand, my trusty fiere,
And gie's a hand o' thine;
And we'll tak a right guid-willie waught,
For auld lang syne.

And surely ye'll be your pint-stowp,
And surely I'll be mine;
And we'll tak a cup o' kindness yet
For auld lang syne.

> For *auld lang syne, my dear.*
> For *auld lang syne,*
> We'll *tak a cup o' kindness yet,*
> For *auld lang syne.*

Robert Burns

I'm Glad

I'm glad the sky is painted blue,
And earth is painted green,
With such a lot of nice fresh air
All sandwiched in between.

Anon.

Index of First Lines

Index of First Lines

Index of First Lines

Index of Poets

Index of Poets

Acknowledgements

The publishers wish to thank the following for permission to use copyright material:

John Agard, 'My Rabbit', First Morning' and 'Secret' from *Another Day on Your Foot*, by permission of Caroline Sheldon Literary Agency on behalf of the author; Allan Ahlberg, 'Bedtime' from *Please Mrs Butler*, Kestrel Books, 1983, p. 93. Copyright © Allan Ahlberg 1983; 'Registration' and 'Billy McBone' from *Heard it in the Playground*, Viking, 1989, pp. 11-12, 32-3. Copyright © Allan Ahlberg, 1989, by permission of Penguin UK; Dorothy Aldis, 'The Island' from *Hop, Skip and Jump!*, Copyright © 1934, renewed © 1961 by Dorothy Aldis, by permission of G P Putnam & Sons, a division of Penguin Putnam Inc; W H Auden, 'Night Mail' and 'Tell me the truth about love' from *Collected Poems*, by permission of Faber and Faber Ltd; Hilaire Belloc, 'The Microbe', 'Matilda', 'Tarantella' and an extract from 'The South Country' from *Complete Verse*, Random House UK, by permission of The Peters Fraser and Dunlop Group Ltd on behalf of the Estate of the author; Gerard Benson, 'A Tale of Two Citizens' from *Does W Trouble You?*, Viking/Puffin Books, by permission of the author; James Berry, 'Okay, Brown Girl, Okay' and 'The Barkday Party' from *Fish Lines*, by permission of Peters Fraser & Dunlop Group Ltd on behalf of the author; Clare Bevan, 'Just Doing My Job', by permission of the author; Valerie Bloom, 'Fruits' from *Duppy Jamboree*, 1992, by permission of Cambridge University Press; and 'Haircut Rap', by permission of the author; N M Boedecker, 'Hippopotamus' from *Snowman Sniffles*, by permission of Faber and Faber Ltd; Vera Brittain, 'Perhaps...', by permission of her literary executors; George Mackay Brown, 'A Child's Calendar' from *Selected Poems*, by permission of John Murray (Publishers) Ltd; Alan Brownjohn, 'We are going to see the rabbit'. Copyright © Alan Brownjohn1959, 1987, 'Explorer'. Copyright © Alan Brownjohn, 1969, 1997; 'Cat'. Copyright © Alan Brownjohn 1970, 1998, by permission of Rosica Colin Ltd on behalf of the author; Charles Causley, 'My Mother Saw a Dancing Bear', 'There Once Was a Man', 'I Had a Little Cat', 'When I Was a Hundred and Twenty Six', 'Give Me a House' and 'The Reverend Sabine Baring-Gould' from *Selected Poems for Children*, Macmillan, by permission of David Higham Associates on behalf of the author; Leonard Clark, 'Montana Born' and 'August Ends', by permission of Robert Clark, Literary Executor of the author; Debjani Chatterjee, 'My Sari', by permission of the author; David Clayton, 'A Parroty of a Poem', by permission of the author; John Coldwell, 'The New Computerised Timetable' and 'I Think My Teacher is a Cowboy', by permission of the author; Paul Cookson, 'Coolscorin'Matchwinnin'Celebratin'Striker!', 'Superman's Dog', 'Wizard with the Ball' and 'The Day After The Day After Boxing

Acknowledgements

Day', by permission of the author; **Wendy Cope**, 'The Uncertainty of the Poet' and 'Telling' from *Another Day on Your Foot*, Macmillan, by permission of Peters Fraser & Dunlop Group Ltd on behalf of the author; **Pie Corbett**, 'Smelling Rats' from *Rice, Pie and Moses*, Macmillan Children's Books. Copyright © Pie Corbett, 1995, 'The Playground Monster' and 'Poetman', by permission of the author; **e e cummings**, 'maggie and milly and molly and may', from *Complete Poems 1904–62*, ed. George J Firmage. Copyright © 1991 by the Trustees for the e e cummings Trust and George James Firmage, by permission of W W Norton & Company Ltd; **John Cunliffe**, 'Fish' from *Pets and Friends*, by permission of David Higham Associates on behalf of the author; **W H Davies**, 'The Happy Child', Jonathan Cape, by permission of Random House UK on behalf of the Executors of the Estate of the author; **Jan Dean**, 'Angels', by permission of the author; **Peter Dixon**, 'Why?', 'Lone Mission' and 'Magic Cat' from *Peter Dixon's Gran Prix of Poetry*, Macmillan forthcoming, and 'Where do all the teachers go?', by permission of the author; **Lord Alfred Douglas**, 'The Shark', by permission of Sheila Colman, Executor of the Literary Estate of the author; **John Drinkwater**, 'Moonlit Apples', by permission of Samuel French Ltd on behalf of the Estate of the author; **Carol Ann Duffy**, 'Mrs Tilscher's Class' from *The Other Country*, 1990, by permission of Anvil Press Poetry; 'The Piano', 'Sharp Freckles' and 'Chocs', by permission of the author; **Richard Edwards**, 'Littlemouse' and 'The Word Party', by permission of the author; **T S Eliot**, 'Macavity: the Mystery Cat' from *Old Possum's Book of Practical Cats*. Copyright © 1939 by T S Eliot and renewed 1967 by Esme Valerie Eliot, by permission of Faber and Faber Ltd; **U A Fanthorpe**, 'What the Donkey Saw' from *Poems for Christmas*, 1982, by permission of Peterloo Poets; **Eleanor Farjeon**, 'Cats', 'Morning Has Broken', Argos and Ulysees', 'It Was Long Ago', 'Sent a Letter to My Love' and 'Carol of the Signs' from *Blackbird Has Spoken*, 'Easter Monday' from *Scars Upon My Heart*, by permission of David Higham Associates on behalf of the Estate of the author; **Aileen Fisher**, 'My Puppy' from *Up the Windy Hill*. Copyright © 1953 Abelard Press, renewed © 1981 by Aileen Fisher; and 'The Furry Ones' from *Feathered Ones and Furry*. Copyright © 1971 by Aileen Fisher, by permission of Marian Reiner on behalf of the author; **Robert Frost**, 'Stopping by Woods on a Snowy Evening', 'The Pasture', 'The Runaway' and 'The Road Not Taken' from *The Poetry of Robert Frost*, ed. Edward Connery Lathem, Jonathan Cape, by permission of Random House; **Rose Fyleman**, 'Mice', by permission of The Society of Authors as the Literary Representative of the Estate of the author; **Carmen de Gasztold**, 'The Prayer of the Little Ducks' from *Prayers from the Ark*, trans. Rumer Godden, 1963, by permission of Macmillan Children's Books; **Kenneth Grahame**, 'Song for Mr Toad' from *The Wind in the Willows*. Copyright © The University Chest, Oxford, by permission of Curtis Brown Ltd on behalf of The University Chest, Oxford; **Robert Graves**, 'I'd Love To Be A Fairy's Child' from

Acknowledgements

Complete Poems, by permission of Carcanet Press; **David Greygoose**, for 'It's Only the Storm', first published in *Language in Colour*, ed. Moira Andrew, Belair, 1989, by permission of the author; **Philip Gross**, 'A Bad Case of Fish' and 'Daughter of the Sea' from *All-Nite Cafe*, by permission of Faber and Faber Ltd; **Mike Harding**, 'Christmas Market' from *Buns For The Elephants*, Viking, 1995, p.23. Copyright © Mike Harding 1995; **Thomas Hardy**, 'The Fallow Deer at the Lonely House' from *The Complete Poems by Thomas Hardy*, ed. James Gibson, Papermac, by permission of Macmillan General Books; **David Harmer**, 'My Mum's Put Me On The Transfer List' and 'What Mountains Do', by permission of the author; **Trevor Harvey**, 'The Painting Lesson' from *The Usborne Book of Children's Poems*, ed. Heather Amery, 1990, by permission of the author; **Maureen Haselhurst**, 'Christmas at Four Winds Farm', by permission of the author; **Seamus Heaney**, 'Blackberry Picking' and 'The Railway Children' from *New Selected Poems 1966-1987*. Copyright © 1990 by Seamus Heaney, by permission of Faber and Faber Ltd; **John Hegley**, 'On the Pavement', by permission of The Peters Fraser and Dunlop Group Ltd on behalf of the author; **Theresa Heine**, 'The Lonely Dragon', by permission of the author; **Stewart Henderson**, 'Soarfish the Swordfish' and 'Octopus or Octopuss', by permission of the author; **Diana Hendry**, 'The Spare Room' from *Strange Goings On*, Penguin Books, 1994. Copyright © 1994 Diana Hendry, by permission of Rogers Coleridge and White Ltd on behalf of the author; **Adrian Henri**, 'Early Spring' and 'Rover' from *The Phantom Lollipop Lady*, Methuen Books, 1986. Copyright © Adrian Henri 1986, 'A Poem for My Cat' from *One of Your Legs*, Macmillan, 1994. Copyright © Adrian Henri 1994; and 'Autumn' from *Dinner With the Spratts*, Methuen Books,1993. Copyright © Adrian Henri 1993, by permission of Rogers, Coleridge and White Ltd on behalf of the author; **Phoebe Hesketh**, 'Sally' and 'Cats', Bodley Head, by permission of Random House UK; **Russell Hoban**, 'October Tuesday', by permission of David Higham Associates on behalf of the author; **Mary Ann Hoberman**, 'Brother' from *Hello and Good-bye*, Little Brown & Co. Copyright © 1959, renewed © 1987 by Mary Ann Hoberman, by permission of Gina Maccoby Literary Agency on behalf of the author; **A E Housman**, 'Loveliest of trees, the cherry now' from *The Shropshire Lad*, by permission of The Society of Authors as the literary representative of the Estate of the author; **Langston Hughes**, 'April Rain Song' and 'Hope' from *The Collected Poems of Langston Hughes*, Vintage, US, by permission of David Higham Associates on behalf of the author; **Ted Hughes**, 'Cow' and 'Stickleback' from *The Cat and the Cuckoo*, by permission of Faber & Faber Ltd; **Elizabeth Jennings**, 'Awake in the Siesta', 'The Smell of the Chrysanthemums', 'Clouds' and 'Autumn' from *A Spell of Words*, Macmillan, by permission of David Higham Associates on behalf of the author; **Jenny Joseph**, 'Warning' from *Selected Poems*, Bloodaxe Books Ltd. Copyright © Jenny Joseph 1992, by permission of John Johnson (Literary Agent)

Acknowledgements

Ltd on behalf of the author; and 'Poem for a Country Child', by permission of the author; **Mike Jubb**, 'Camilla Caterpillar', by permission of the author; **Jackie Kay**, 'Brendon Gallacher', Mr and Mrs Lilac', 'Dracula' and 'Divorce', by permission of the author; **Jean Kenward**, 'Dragon', by permission of the author; **Rudyard Kipling**, 'If' and 'The Way Through the Woods', by permission of A P Watt Ltd on behalf of The National Trust; **Philip Larkin**, 'Days' from *Collected Poems*, by permission of Faber and Faber Ltd; **D H Lawrence**, 'Little Fish' from *The Complete Poems of D H Lawrence*, ed. V de Sola Pinto and F W Roberts. Copyright © 1964, 1971 by Angelo Ravagli and C M Weekley, Executors of the Estate of Frieda Lawrence Ravagli, by permission of Laurence Pollinger Ltd on behalf of the Estate of Frieda Lawrence Ravagli; **Brian Lee**, 'New Shoes' by permission of the author and 'Our Bonfire' from *Late Home*, Kestrel, 1976. Copyright © Brian Lee 1976, by permission of Penguin UK; **Jean Little**, 'Today' from *Hey World, Here I Am!* Copyright © 1986 by Jean Little, by permission of Kids Can Press Ltd, Toronto; **Roger McGough**, 'No Peas for the Wicked', 'First Day at School', 'The Sound Collector' and 'Flight of the Year' from *You Tell Me*, Viking Kestrel, and 'Valentine Poem' from *Sky in the Pie*, Viking Kestrel, by permission of Peters Fraser and Dunlop Group Ltd on behalf of the author; **Ian McMillan**, 'Can't be bothered to think of a title', 'This Little Poem' and 'Ten Things Found in a Wizard's Pocket', by permission of the author; **Colin McNaughton**, 'The Garden's Full of Witches' and 'Permit Holders Only' from *There's An Awful Lot of Weirdos in Our Neighbourhood*. Copyright © 1987 Colin McNaughton; 'Mum is Having a Baby' from *Who's Been Sleeping in My Porridge*. Copyright © Colin McNaughton, by permission of Walker Books Ltd; **Lindsay MacRae**, '2 Poems for 4 Eyes' and 'The Boy Who Dropped Litter' from *You Canny Shove Your Granny Off a Bus*, Viking, 1995. Copyright © Lindsay MacRae 1995, by permission of The Agency (London) Ltd on behalf of the author; **Wes Magee**, 'The Meadow in Midsummer', 'At the End of a School Day', 'Instructions for the last day in October' and 'Footballers in the Park' from *Matt, Wes and Pete*, by permission of the author; **Michelle Magorian**, 'Rushing' from *Orange Paw Marks*, Viking, 1991, p. 27. Copyright © Michelle Magorian, 1991, by permission of Penguin UK; **Walter de la Mare**, 'The Listeners', 'Tartary' and 'Silver' from *The Complete Poems of Walter de la Mare*, 1969, by permission of the Literary Trustees of the author and The Society of Authors as their representative; **John Masefield**, 'Cargoes' and 'Sea Fever', by permission of The Society of Authors as the literary representative of the Estate of the author; **Spike Milligan**, 'Today I saw a little worm', 'Bump' and 'I'm not frightened of pussy cats', by permission of Spike Milligan Productions Ltd; **Trevor Millum**, 'Here is the Feather Warcast' and 'Puma', by permission of the author; **A A Milne**, 'The Three Little Foxes' from *When We Were Very Young'*, Methuen Children's Books, 'Forgiven' from *Now We Are Six*, Methuen Children's Books, by permission of Egmont Children's Books

Acknowledgements

Ltd; **Adrian Mitchell**, 'Patchwork Rap' and 'Nothingmas Day' from *Balloon Lagoon and the Magic Islands of Poetry*, Orchard Books, 1997. © Adrian Mitchell, by permission of The Peters Fraser and Dunlop Group Ltd on behalf of the author (Educational Health Warning! Adrian Mitchell asks that none of his poems are used in connection with any examinations whatsoever.); **Tony Mitton**, 'I Wanna Be A Star' from *Plum*, Scholastic. Copyright © Tony Mitton 1998, by permission of David Higham Associates on behalf of the author. **Harold Monro**, 'Overheard on a Salt Marsh' from *Collected Poems*, by permission from Gerald Duckworth and Company Ltd; **Brian Moses**, 'What Teachers Wear in Bed and 'Aliens Stole My Underpants', by permission of the author; **Ogden Nash**, 'The Duck' © 1940, 'The Cow' © 1939 and 'The Octopus' © 1941 from *The Ogden Nash Pocket Book*, Pocket Books. Copyright © by Ogden Nash, renewed, by permission of Curtis Brown, Ltd on behalf of the Estate of the author; **Judith Nicholls**, 'SS Titanic' from *Storm's Eye*, Oxford University Press. Copyright © Judith Nicholls 1994; 'Lines' from *Magic Mirror*, Faber and Faber. Copyright © Judith Nicholls 1995; and 'Breakfast for One'. Copyright © Judith Nicholls 1986, by permission of the author; **Grace Nichols**, 'Come on into my Tropical Garden', 'Early Country Village Morning' from *Come On Into My Tropical Garden*, 'Morning' and Give Yourself a Hug' from *Give Yourself a Hug*, and 'Don't Cry Caterpillar' from *No Hickory No Dickory No Dock*. Copyright © Grace Nichols 1988, 1994, 1991, by permission of Curtis Brown Ltd on behalf of the author; **Alfred Noyes**, 'Daddy Fell in the Pond' from *Collected Poems*, by permission of John Murray (Publishers) Ltd; **Jack Ousbey**, 'Gran, Can You Rap', by permission of the author; **Gareth Owen**, 'Can We Have Our Ball Back Please?' and 'Schoolgirl on a Train' from *The Fox on the Roundabout*, Young Lions, 1985, 'The Owl and the Astronaut' from *Song of the City*, HarperCollins, 1985, and 'Moon' from *My Granny is a Sumo Wrestler*, Methuen Books, 1994. Copyright © Gareth Owen 1985, 1994, by permission of Rogers, Coleridge & White Ltd on behalf of the author; **Brian Patten**, 'You Can't Be That', 'Burying the Dog in the Garden', 'Dear Mum' and 'Gust Becos I Cud Not Spel' from *Thawing Frozen Frogs*, Viking, 1990. Copyright © Brian Patten 1990; 'A Small Dragon' from *Notes to the Hurrying Man*, Allen & Unwin, 1980. Copyright © 1980, 'Mr McGuire' from *The Utter Nutters*, Viking, 1994. Copyright © Brian Patten 1994, by permission of Rogers, Coleridge and White on behalf of the author; **Gervase Phinn**, 'Creative Writing', by permission of the author; **Christopher Pilling**, 'The Meeting Place' from *Poems for Christmas*, 1982, by permission of Peterloo Poets; **Jack Prelutsky**, 'Countdown' from *It's Halloween*, William Heinemann, by permission of Egmont Children's Books Ltd; **Irene Rawnsley**, 'Purple Shoes', by permission of the author; **James Reeves**, 'Cows', 'Fireworks', 'Spells' and 'Things to Remember' from *Complete Poems for Children*, Heinemann, by permission of Laura Cecil Literary Agency on behalf of the Estate

Acknowledgements

of the author; **John Rice**, 'Dazzledance', 'The Mysteries of Nature', 'Ettykett' and 'If' from *Rice, Pie & Moses*, Macmillan, by permission of the author; **Laura Richards**, 'Eletelephony' from *Tirra Lirra*. Copyright © 1930, 1932 by Laura E Richards, renewed © 1960 by Hamilton Richards, by permission of Little Brown and Company; **E V Rieu**, 'The Paint Box', 'What Does It Matter?' and 'Sir Smashum Uppe', by permission of D C H Rieu, Executor of the Estate of the author; **Theodore Roethke**, 'The Meadow Mouse' from *Collected Poems*, by permission of Faber and Faber Ltd; **Michael Rosen**, 'Busy Day' from *One of Your Legs*, and 'Me and My Brother', from *The Hypnotiser*, André Deutsch Children's Books, an imprint of Scholastic Children's Books. Copyright ©1988 Michael Rosen, by permission of The Peters Fraser and Dunlop Group Ltd on behalf of the author; **A L Rowse**, 'The White Cat of Trenarren', by permission of John Johnson (Authors' Agent) Ltd on behalf of the Estate of the author; **Vernon Scannell**, 'Grannie', by permission of the author; **Fred Sedgwick**, 'Mr Khan's Shop' from *Blind Date*, Tricky Sam! Press, 1997, and 'Girl With a Worksheet in a Castle', by permission of the author; **Danielle Sensier**, 'Experiment' from *Poems About Growth*, Wayland, 1995, by permission of the author; **Dr Seuss**, extract from 'Quack, Quack' from *Oh Say Can You Say*. Copyright © Dr Seuss Enterprises, L P, 1979, by permission of International Creative Management, Inc on behalf of Dr Seuss Enterprises, L P; **Shel Silverstein**, 'It's Dark in Here' from *Where the Sidewalk Ends*. Copyright © 2007 by Evil Eye Music, Inc; by permission of Edite Kroll Literary Agency, Inc on behalf of the author; and HarperCollins Publishers; **Matt Simpson**, 'Walking a Friend's Dog', 'Autumn Gale' and 'In Grandma's Kitchen' from Matt, Wes and Pete, by permission of the au thor; **Marion Simpson**, 'Jess', winner of the Pushkin Prize, 1994, by permission of the author; **Edith Sitwell**, 'Madame Mouse' from Collected Poems, Sinclair-Stevenson, by permission of David Higham Associates on behalf of the author; **James Stephens**, 'In the Orchard', by permission of The Society of Authors as Literary Representative of the Estate of the author; Roger Stevens, 'Walking the dog seems like fun to me', first appeared in Parent Free Zone, Macmillan, by permission of the author; **Matthew Sweeney**, 'Cows on the Beach' and 'All the Dogs' from The Flying Spring Onion, by permission of Faber and Faber Ltd; **Dylan Thomas**, 'The Song of the Mischievous Dog' from The Poems, J M Dent, by permission of David Higham Associates on be half of the Estate of the author; **Nick Toczek**, 'The Dragon in the Cellar', by per mission of the author; **Steve Turner**, 'Burglars' from The King of Twist, by permission of Hodder and Stoughton Ltd; Colin West, 'Geraldine Giraffe', by permission of the author; **Robert Westall**, 'Wind Cat' from Snake on the Bus, ed. Valerie Bierman. Copyright © 1994 The Estate of Robert Westall, by permission of Laura Cecil Liter ary Agency on behalf of the Estate of the author; **Valerie Worth**, 'back yard' from Still More Small Poems. Copyright © 1979 by Valerie Worth, by permission of Farrar, Straus & Giroux, Inc; **Kit Wright**, 'Sergeant Brown's Parrot', 'Watch Your French'

Acknowledgements

and 'The Magic Box', by permission of the author; **W B Yeats**, 'He Wishes for the Cloths of Heaven' and 'An Irishman Foresees His Death' from The Collected Poems of W B Yeats, Vol. I: The Poems, revised and edited by Richard J Finneran. Copyright © 1983, 1989 by Anne Yeats, by permission of A P Watt on behalf of Michael Yeats. Every effort has been made to trace the copyright holders but if any have been inadvertently overlooked the publishers will be pleased to make the necessary arrangement at the first opportunity.

A selected list of Poetry titles available from Macmillan Children's Books

The prices shown below are correct at the time of going to press. However, Macmillan Publishers reserves the right to show new retail prices on covers, which may differ from those previously advertised.

All Pan Macmillan titles can be ordered from our website, www.panmacmillan.com, or from your local bookshop and are also available by post from:

Bookpost, PO Box 29, Douglas, Isle of Man IM99 1BQ
Credit cards accepted. For details:
Telephone: 01624 677237
Fax: 01624 670923
Email: bookshop@enterprise.net
www.bookpost.co.uk

Free postage and packing in the United Kingdom